best of
karrin allyson

Cover photo by Bill Phelps

Transcribed by Forrest "Woody" Mankowski

ISBN 0-634-08782-7

HAL•LEONARD® CORPORATION

7777 W. BLUEMOUND RD. P.O. BOX 13819 MILWAUKEE, WI 53213

Visit Hal Leonard Online at
www.halleonard.com

contents

AND SO IT GOES

Words and Music by
BILLY JOEL

Rubato Ballad

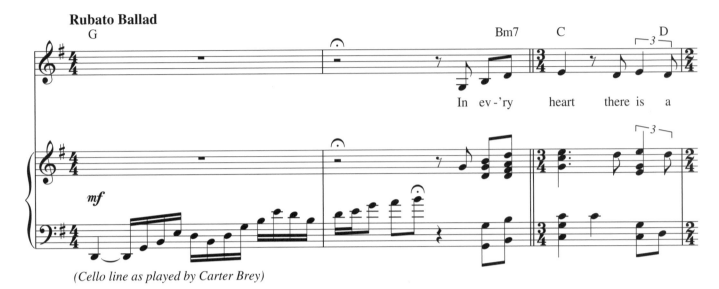

(Cello line as played by Carter Brey)

In ev-'ry heart there is a

room, a sanc-tu-ar-y, safe and strong, to heal the

wounds of lov-ers past un-til a new one comes a-long. ___

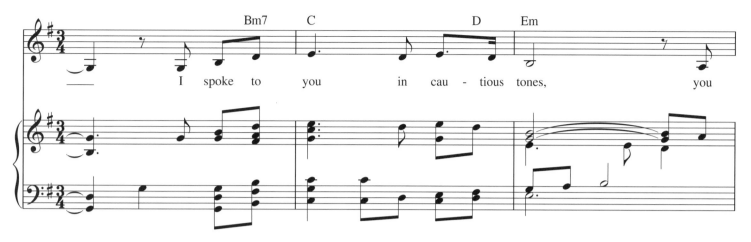

I spoke to you in cau - tious tones, you

an - swered me with no pre - tense, and still I feel I said too

much. My si - lence is my self - de - fense.

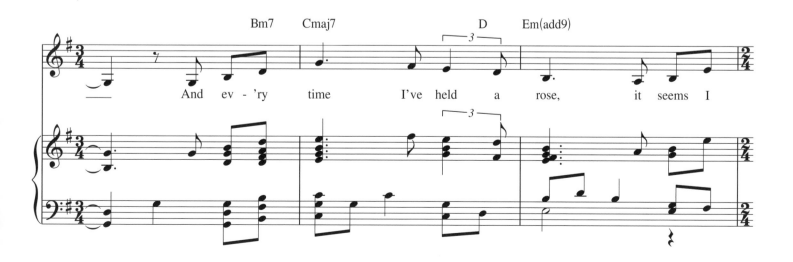

And ev - 'ry time I've held a rose, it seems I

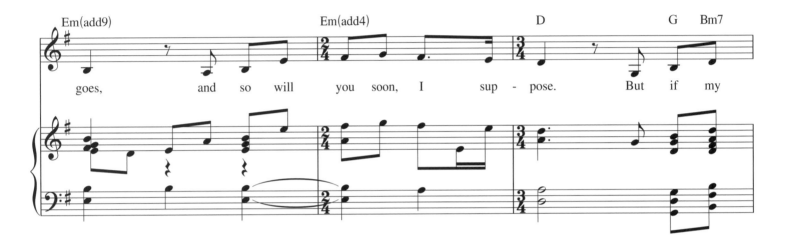

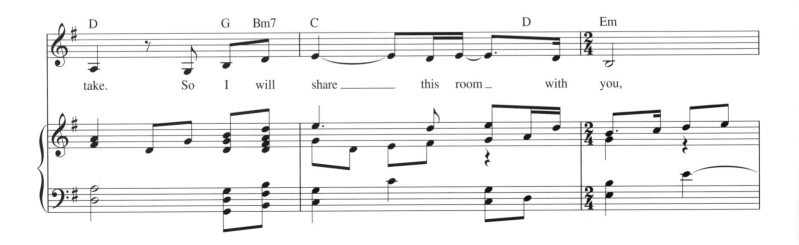

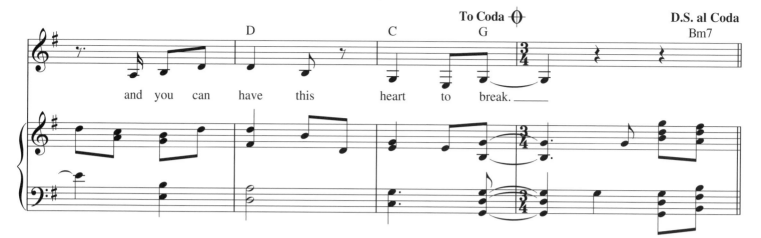

ANGEL EYES

Words by EARL BRENT
Music by MATT DENNIS

Moderate Ballad

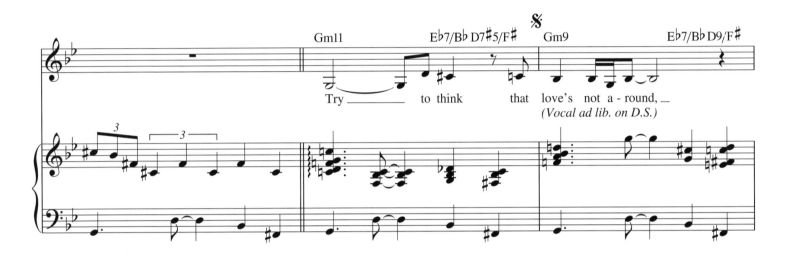

Try _____ to think that love's not a - round, _
(Vocal ad lib. on D.S.)

still it's un - com - forta - bly near. _ My old heart ain't _

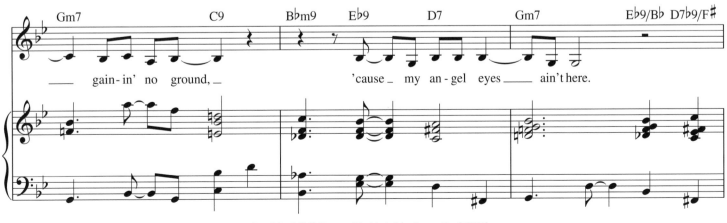

_____ gain - in' no ground, _ 'cause _ my an - gel eyes _____ ain't here.

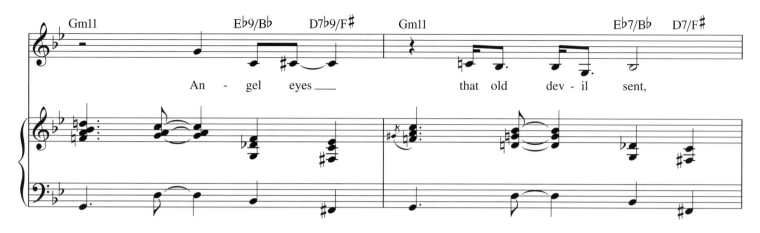

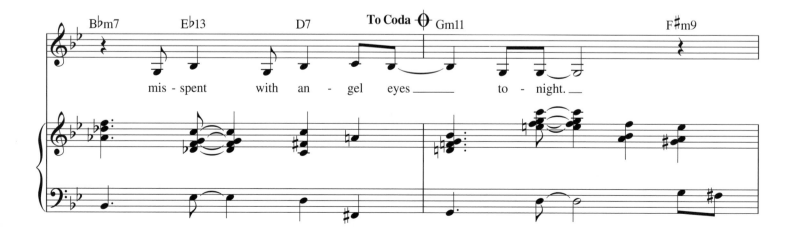

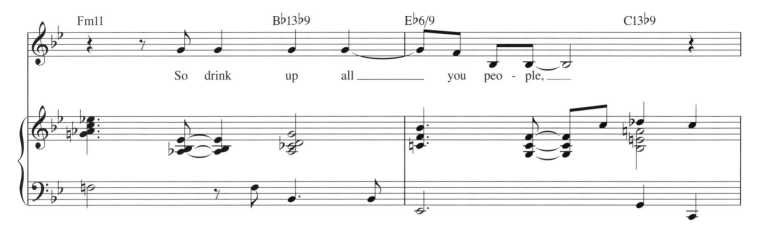

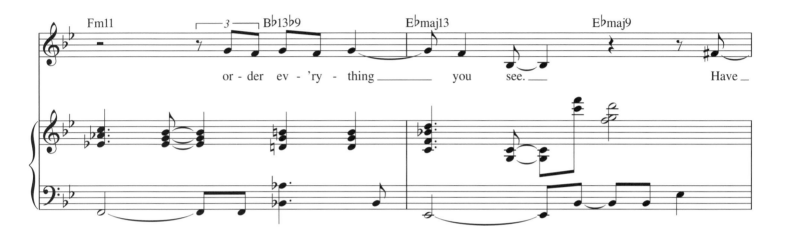

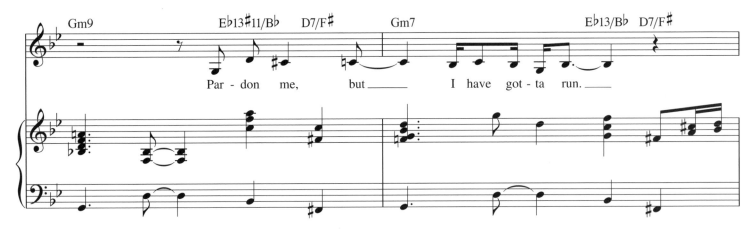

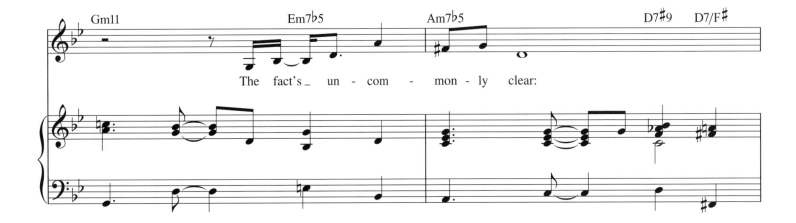

D.S. al Coda

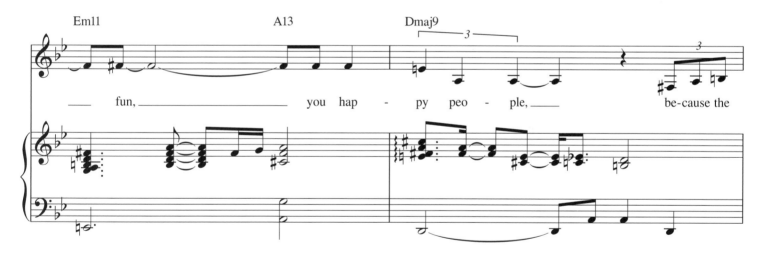

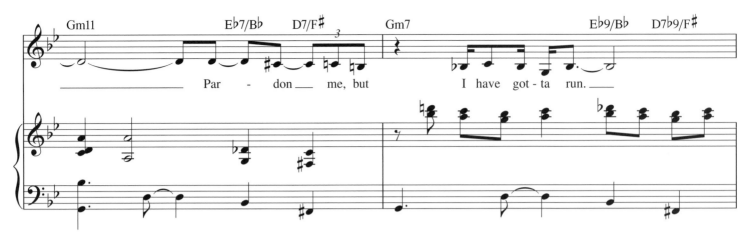

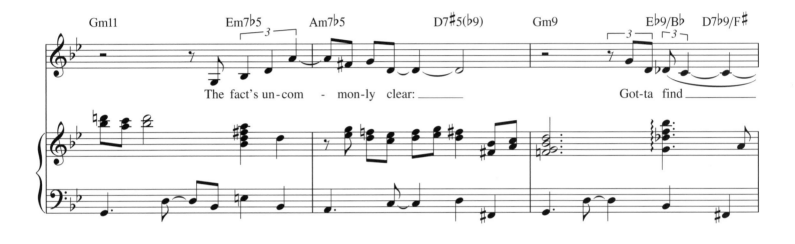

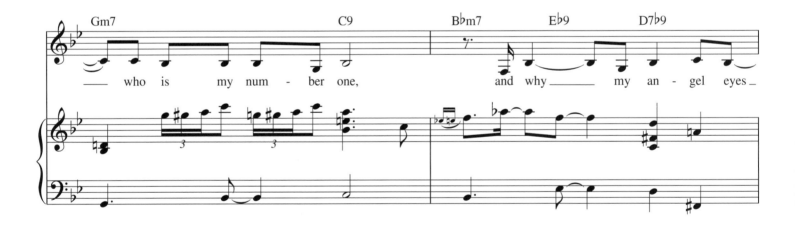

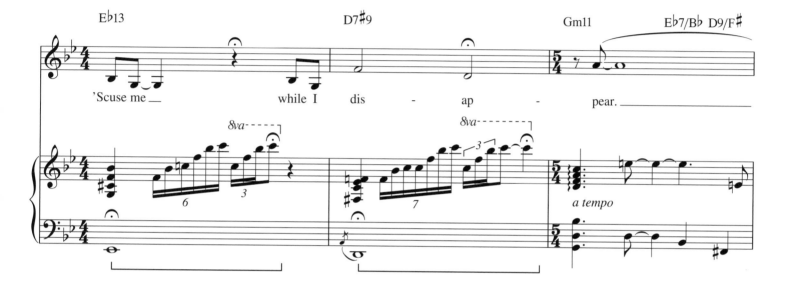

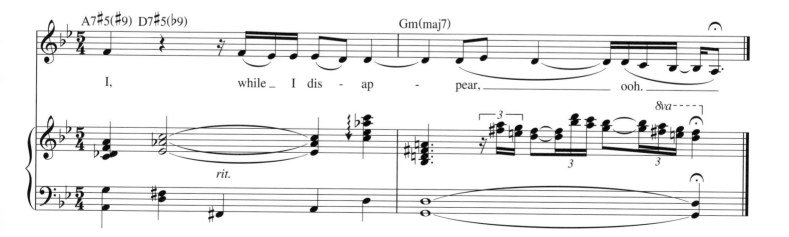

AZURE TÉ
(Paris Blues)

Lyric by DON WOLF
Music by BILL DAVIS

Moderate Swing

Gone ___ and ___ got the ___ blues ___ in Par - is,

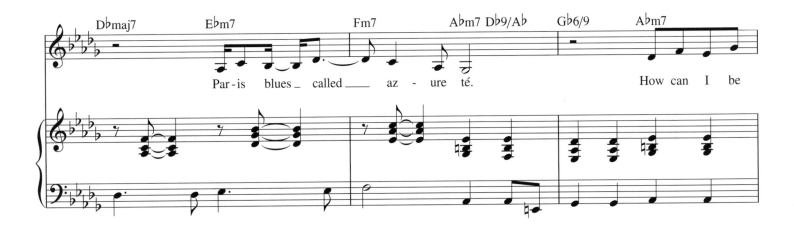

Par - is blues ___ called ___ az - ure té.   How can I be

blue ___ in Par - is? ___   Eas - y ___ when you're far a - way.

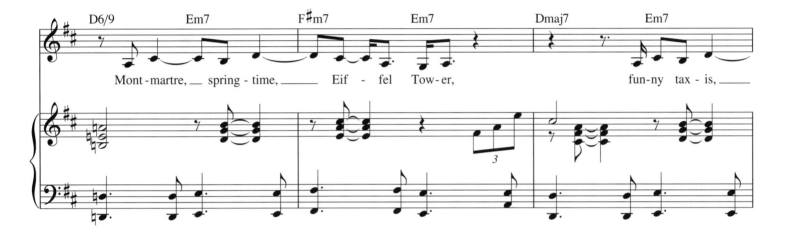

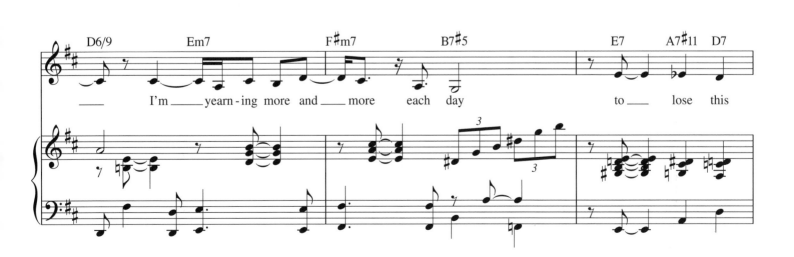

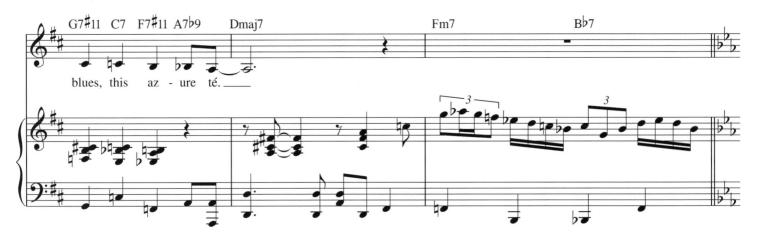

blues, this az - ure té. ____

Repeat 6 times

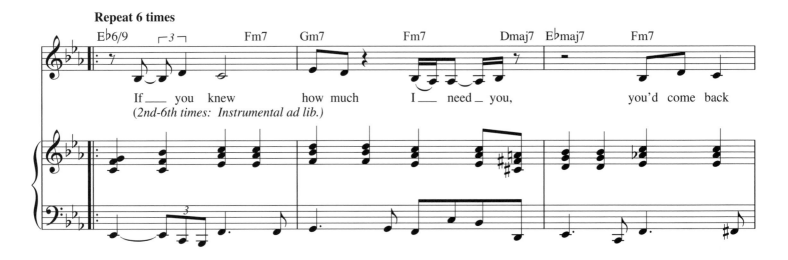

If ____ you knew how much I ____ need ____ you, you'd come back
(2nd-6th times: Instrumental ad lib.)

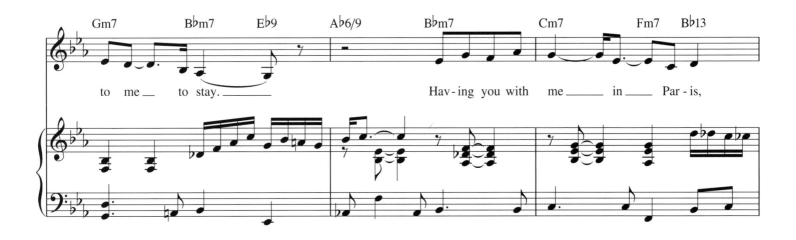

to me ____ to stay. ____ Hav - ing you with me ____ in ____ Par - is,

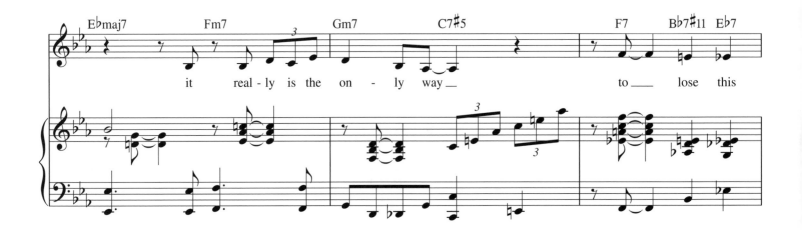

it real - ly is the on - ly way ____ to ____ lose this

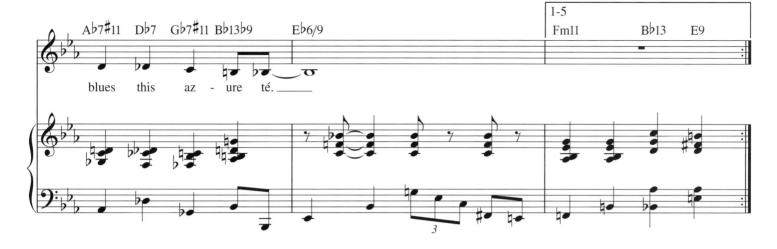

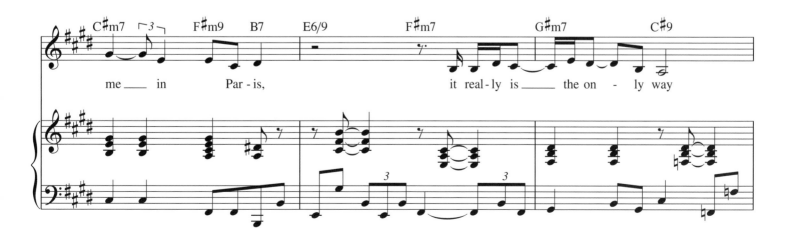

to ___ lose this blues, this az - ure té.

Can't ___ lose this blues, this az - ure té. _____

Can't ___ lose ___ this ___ blues, ___ this ___ az - ure ___

molto rit.

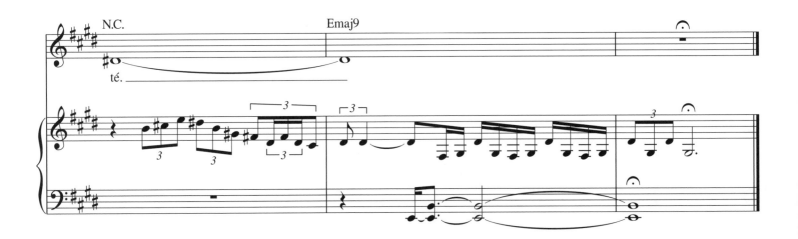

té. _____

BLAME IT ON MY YOUTH

Words by EDWARD HEYMAN
Music by OSCAR LEVANT

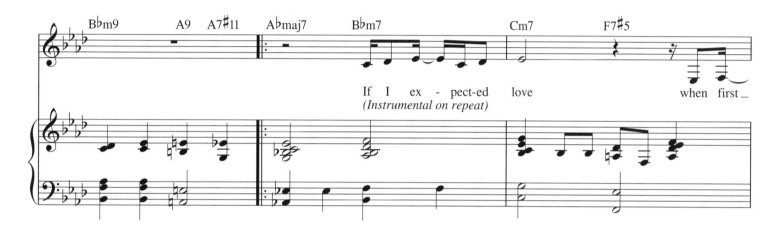

If I ex-pect-ed love
(Instrumental on repeat)
when first

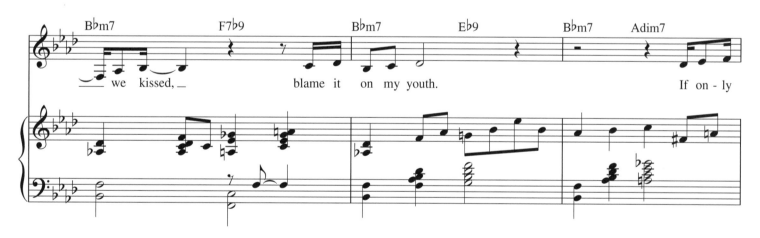

we kissed, _ blame it on my youth.
If on-ly

just for you _ I did ex-ist, _ blame it on my youth.

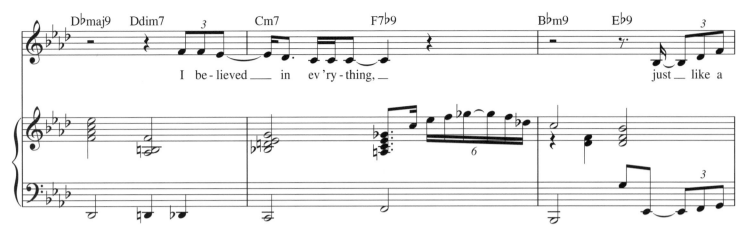

I be-lieved ___ in ev'ry-thing, ___ just ___ like a

child of three. You meant more than an-y-thing,

all ___ the world to me.

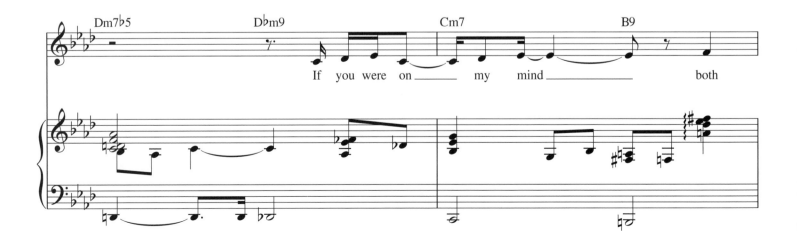

If you were on ___ my mind ___ both

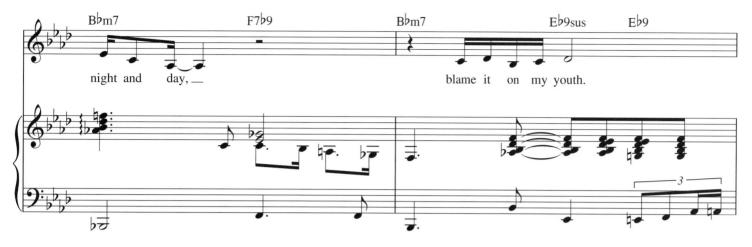

night and day, ___ blame it on my youth.

If I for - got to eat, sleep, ___

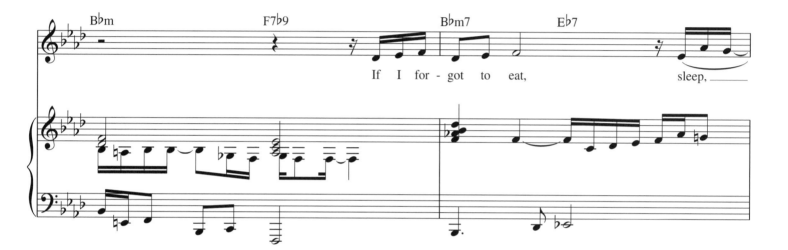

___ and pray, ___ blame it on my ___ youth. ___

If I ___ cried ___ just a ___ lit - tle ___ bit

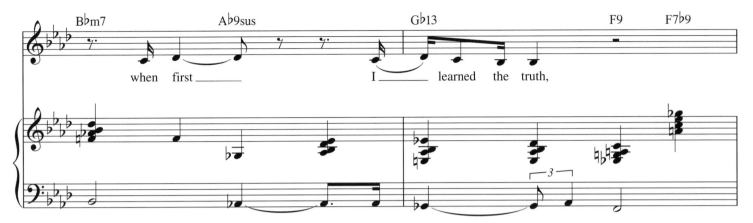

when first _____ I _____ learned the truth,

don't you blame it on my heart, _____

blame it on, _____ blame it on my _____ youth. _____

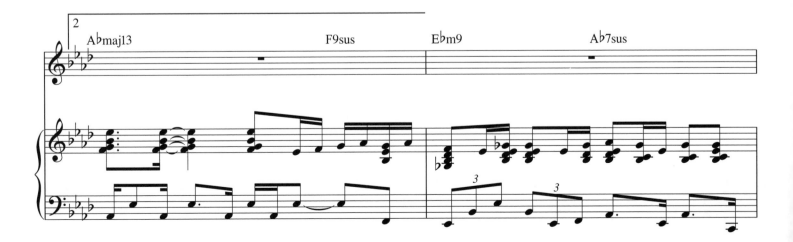

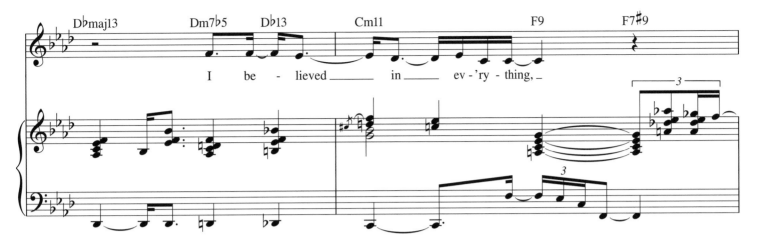

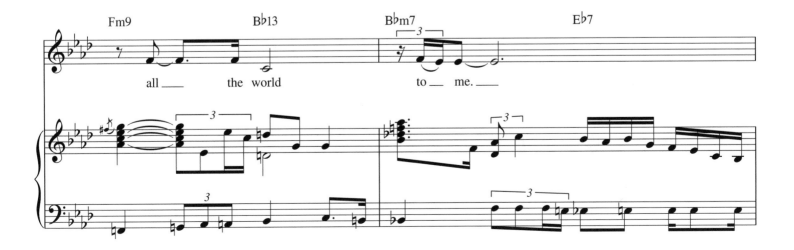

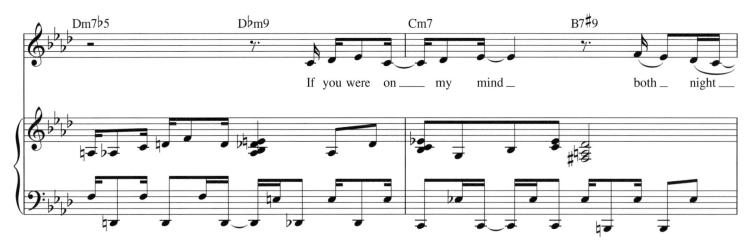

just a ____ lit - tle bit   when first ___ I learn the

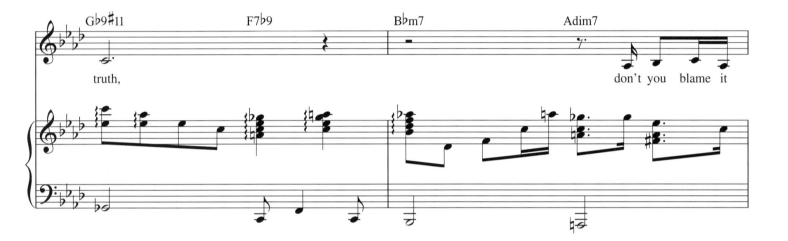

truth,   don't you blame it

on my heart, _   blame it on my youth,   blame _ it __ on _ my

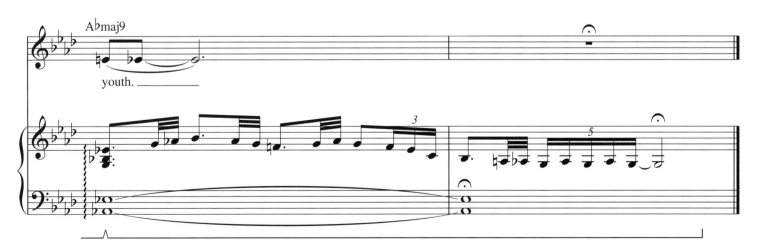

youth. _____

DAY DREAM

Words by JOHN LA TOUCHE
Music by DUKE ELLINGTON
and BILLY STRAYHORN

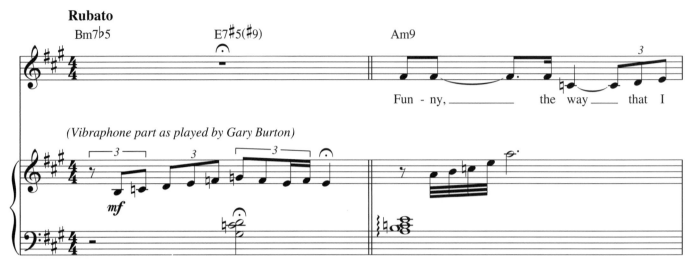

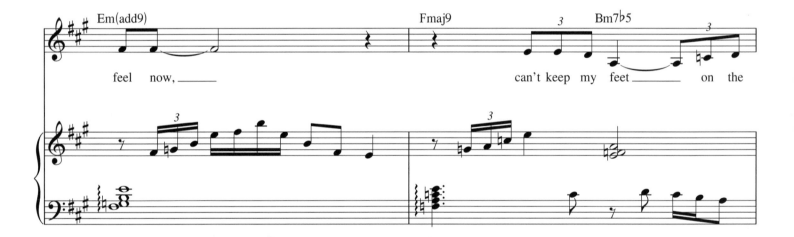

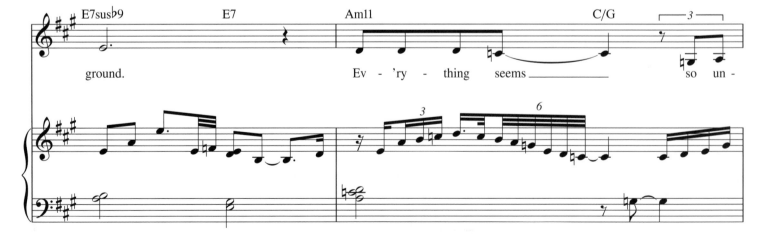

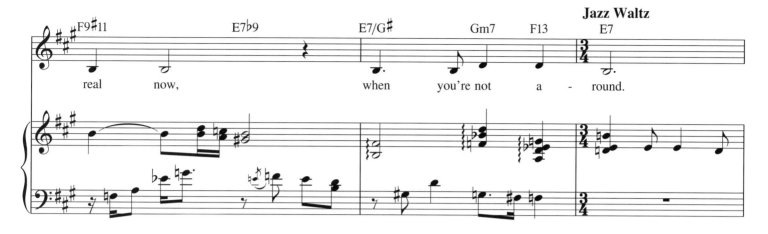

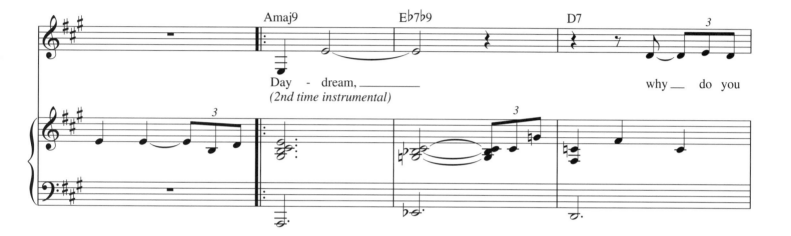

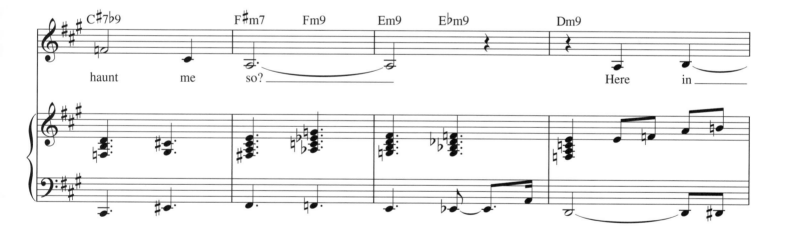

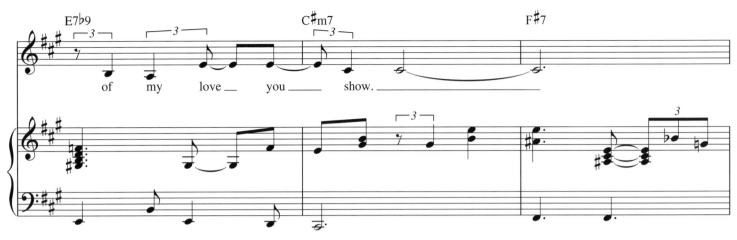

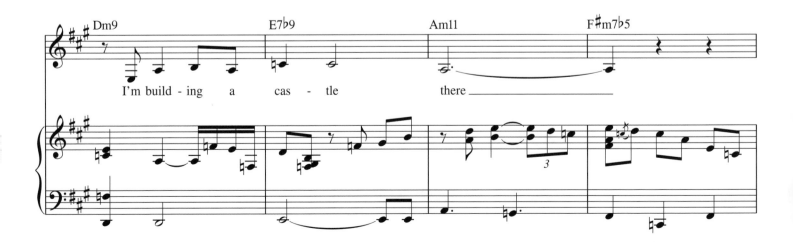

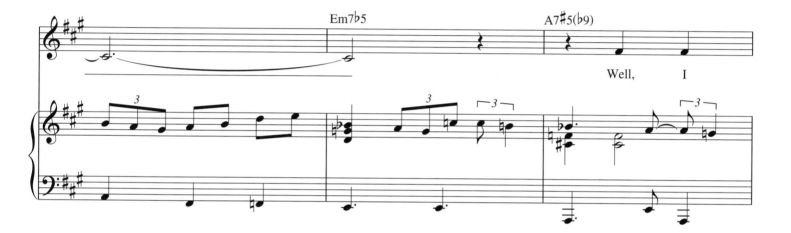

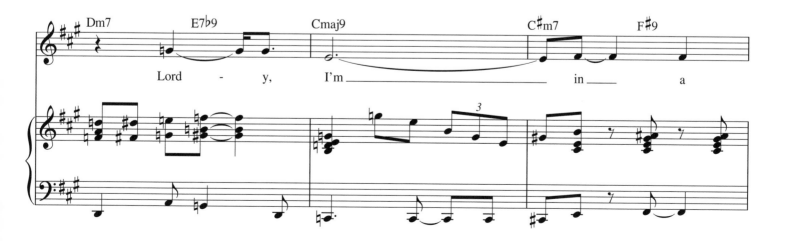

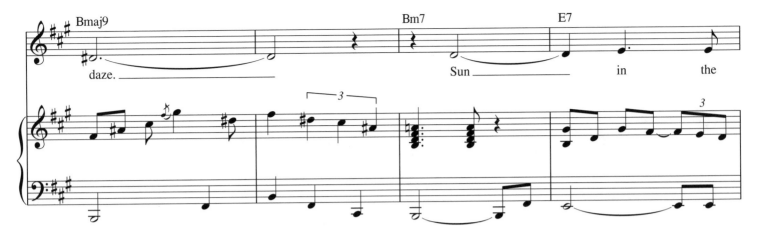

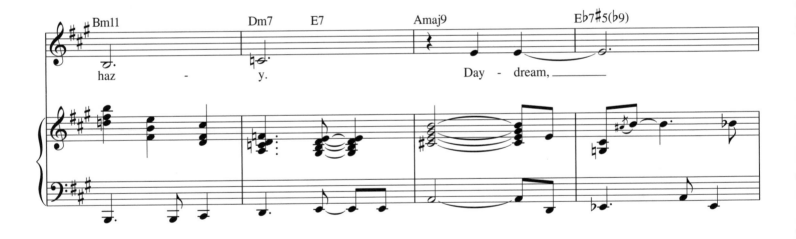

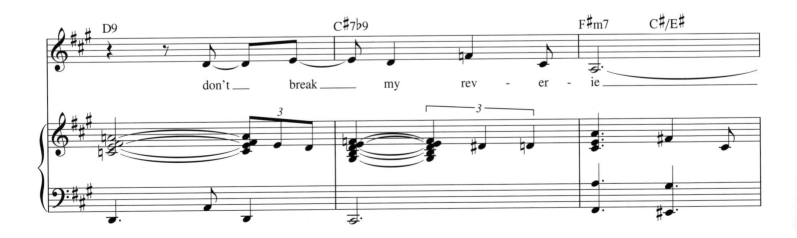

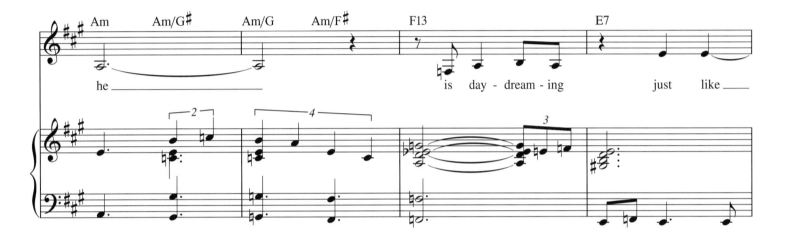

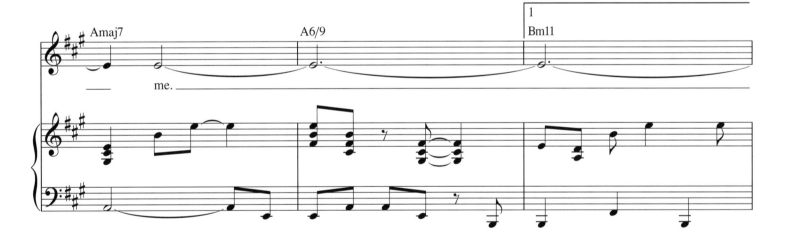

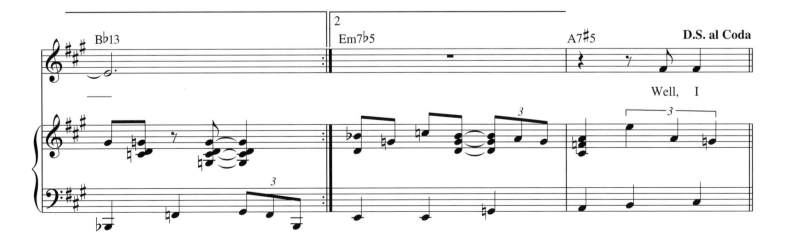

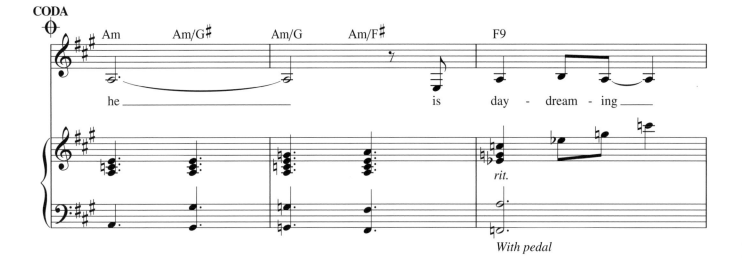

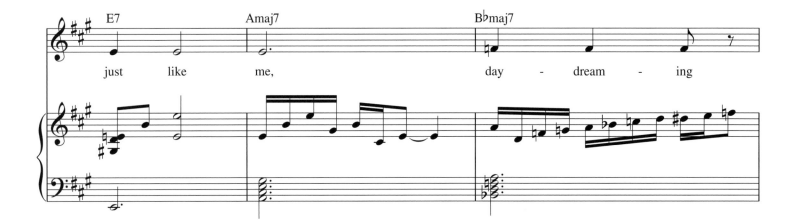

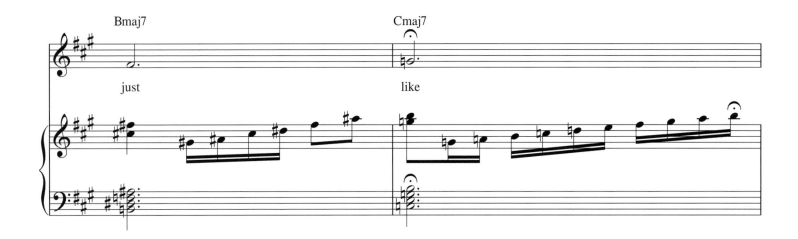

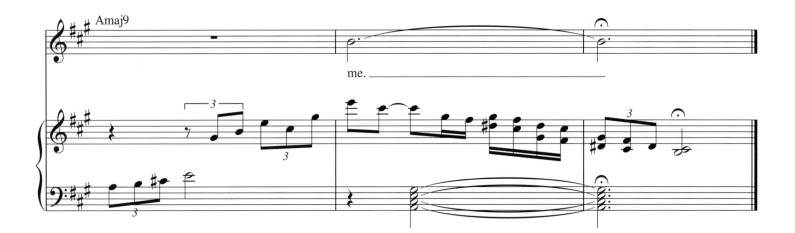

HERE, THERE, AND EVERYWHERE

Words and Music by JOHN LENNON
and PAUL McCARTNEY

Moderate Ballad

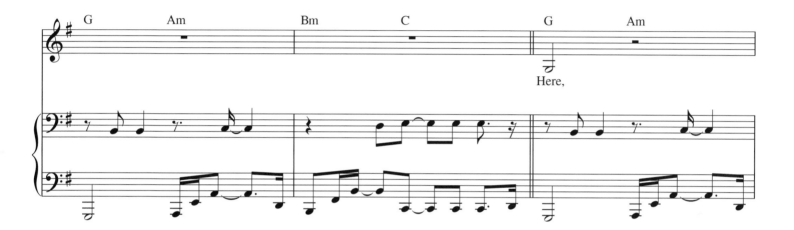

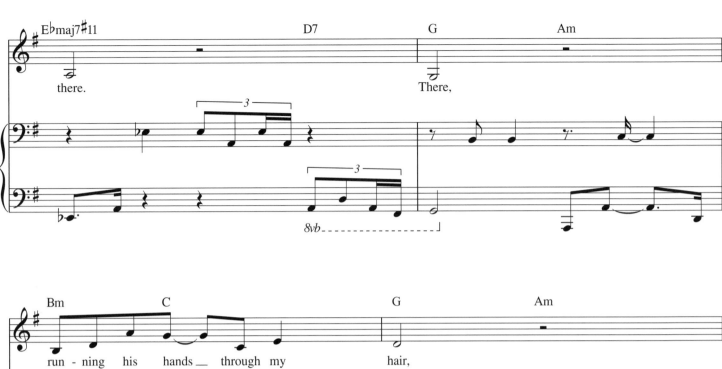

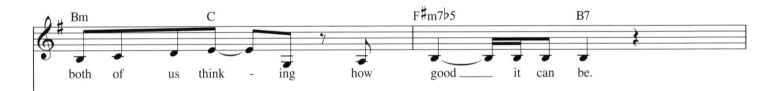

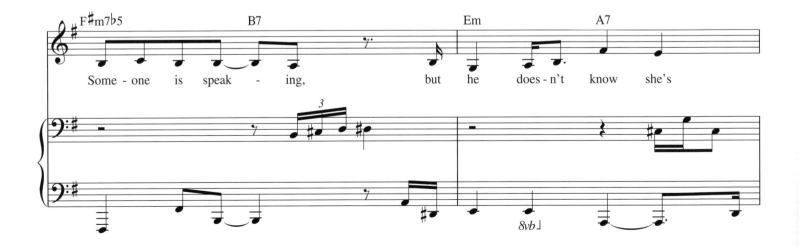

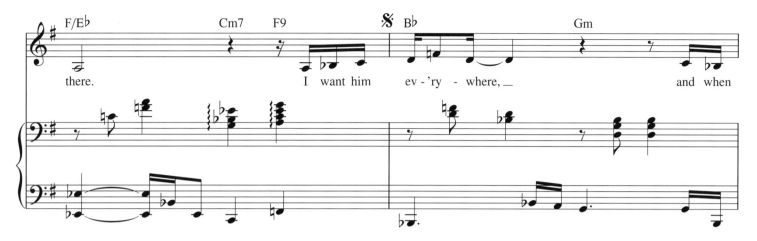

there. I want him ev-'ry-where, __ and when

he's be-side __ me, I know __ I need nev-er __ care,

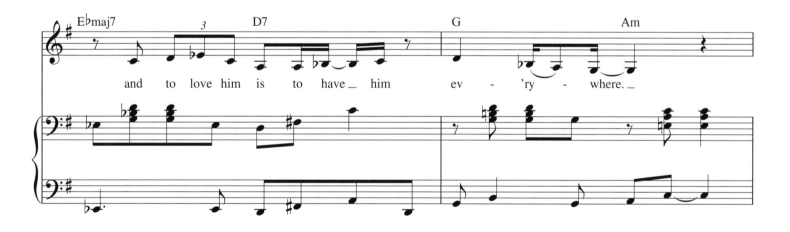

and to love him is to have __ him ev-'ry-where. __

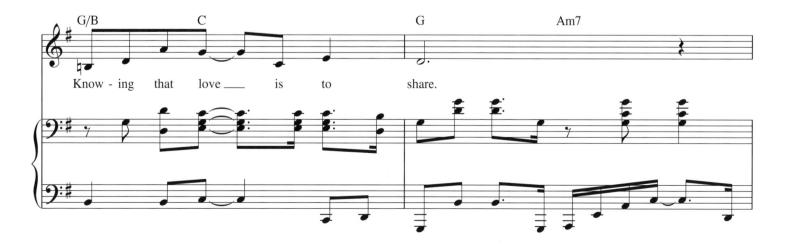

Know-ing that love __ is to share.

Each one be-liev - ing that love nev-er dies. ___

To Coda ⊕

Watch-ing his eyes, ___ and ___ hop-ing he's al - ways ___ there. ___

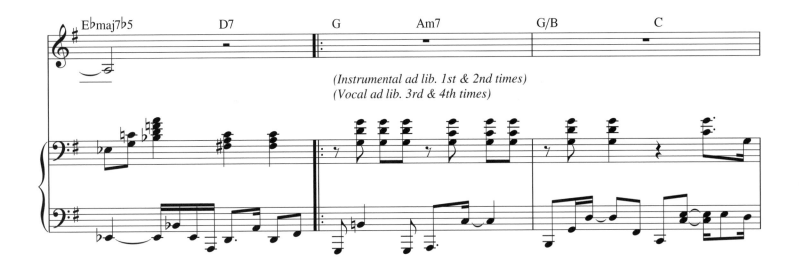

(Instrumental ad lib. 1st & 2nd times)
(Vocal ad lib. 3rd & 4th times)

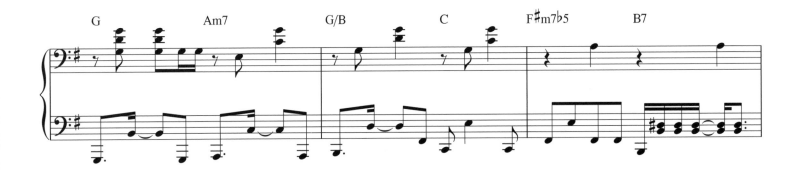

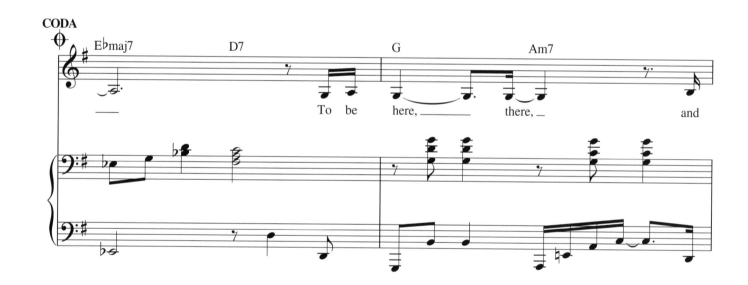

FEEL LIKE MAKIN' LOVE

Words and Music by
EUGENE McDANIELS

Moderate Funk

(Vocal ad lib. 2nd time)

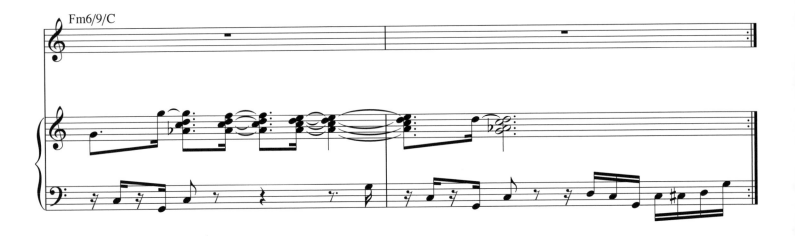

1. Stroll - in' in ___ the park, ___   watch - in' win - ter ___
2. When you talk ___ to me, ___   when you're moan - in'
3. *(Instrumental ad lib. on D.S. until 1st ending)*
4. *(See additional lyrics)*

Fm6/9/C

turn to spring,
sweet and low,

G7susb9

walk-in' _____ in _____ the dark, _____ see-in' lov-
when you're _ touch - in' me _____ and my feel-

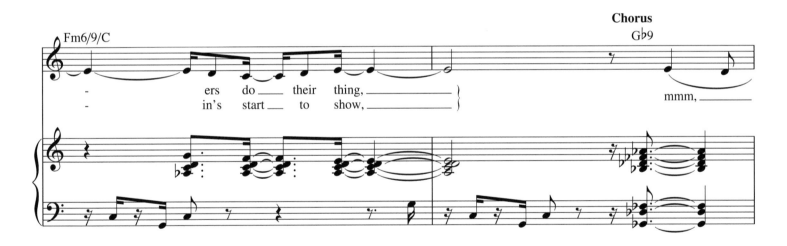

Fm6/9/C

Chorus
Gb9

-ers do _____ their thing, _____
-in's start _____ to show, _____

mmm, _____

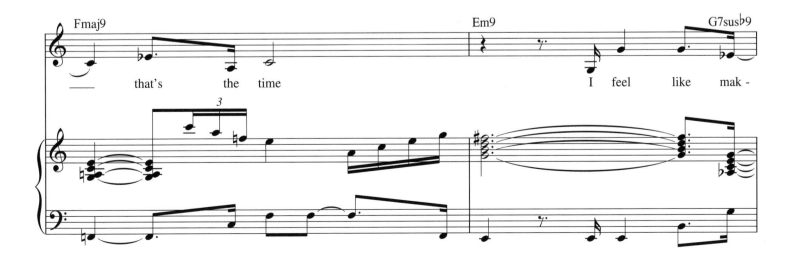

Fmaj9

_____ that's the time

Em9

I feel like mak-

G7susb9

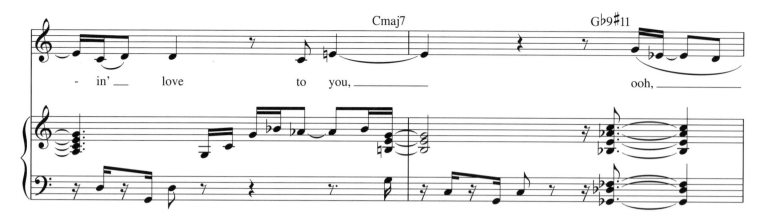

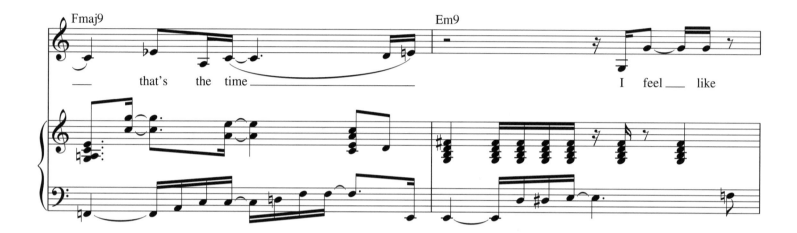

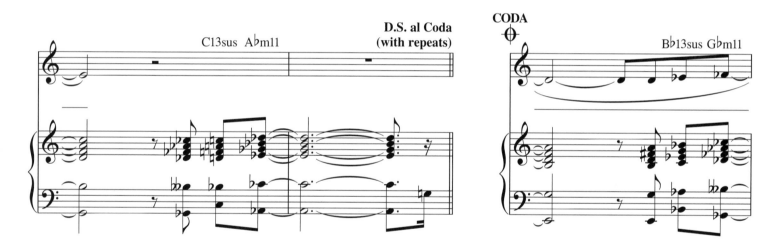

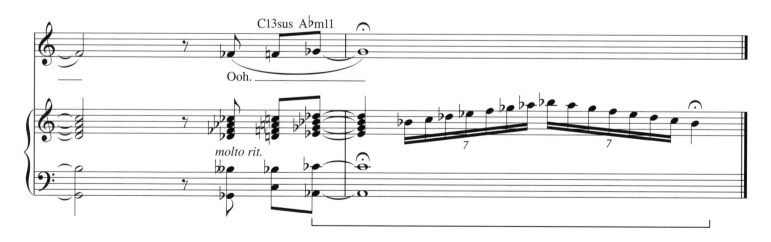

Additional Lyrics

4. In a restaurant,
   Holdin' hands by candlelight,
   While I'm touchin' you,
   Wanting you with all my might,
   Chorus

HOW INSENSITIVE
(Insensatez)

Music by ANTONIO CARLOS JOBIM
Original Words by VINICIUS DE MORAES
English Words by NORMAN GIMBEL
Introduction adapted from Chopin's
Prelude in E Minor, Op. 28, No. 4

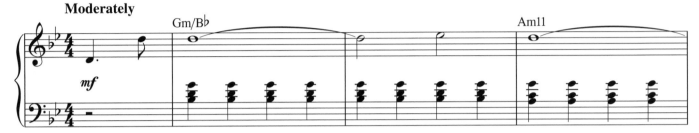

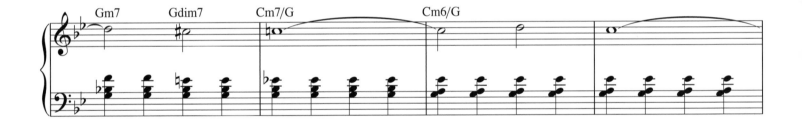

Bossa Nova

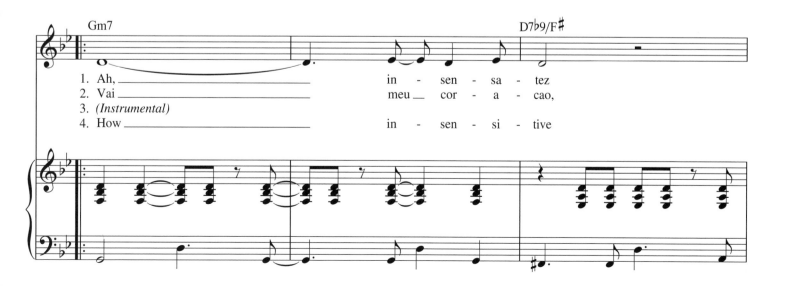

1. Ah, _____ in - sen - sa - tez
2. Vai _____ meu cor - a - cao,
3. *(Instrumental)*
4. How _____ in - sen - si - tive

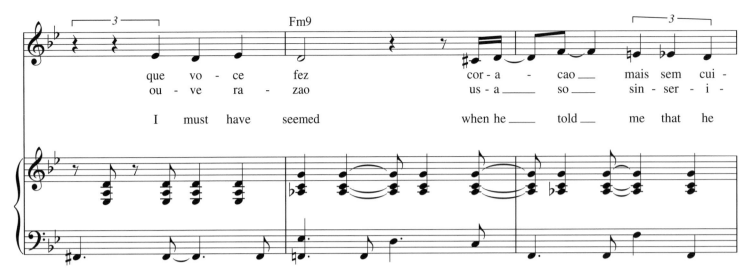

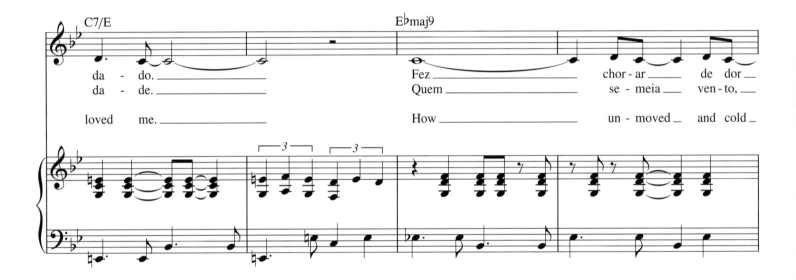

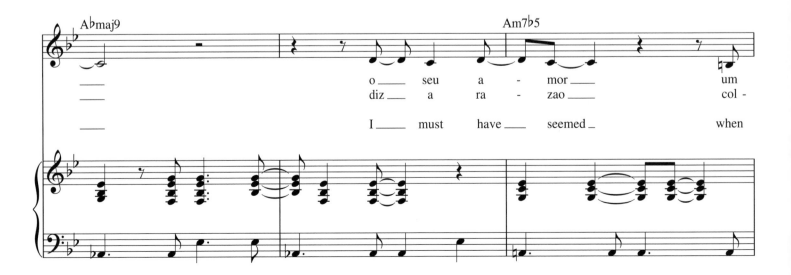

a - mor _____ tao ___ del - i - ca - do. _____
he sem - pre tem - pet - a - de. _____
he told _____ me ___ so sin - cere - ly. _____

Ah, _____ por - que vo - ce _____
Vai _____ meu ___ cor - a - cao _____
Why, _____ he ___ must have ___ asked, ___

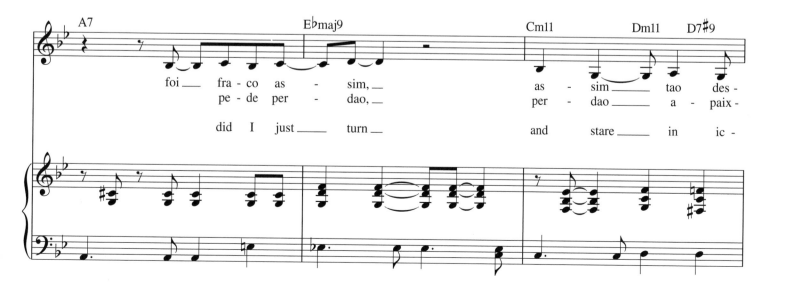

foi ___ fra - co as - sim, ___ as - sim _____ tao des -
pe - de per - dao, ___ per - dao _____ a - paix -
did I just ___ turn ___ and stare _____ in ic -

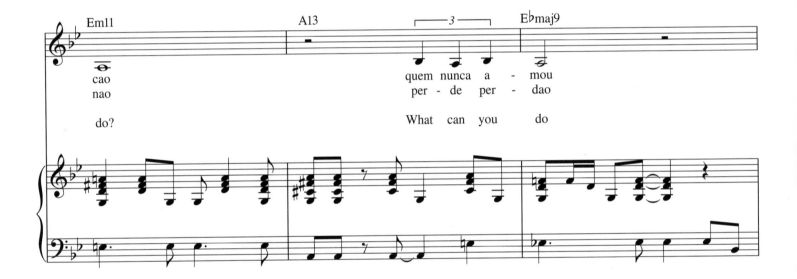

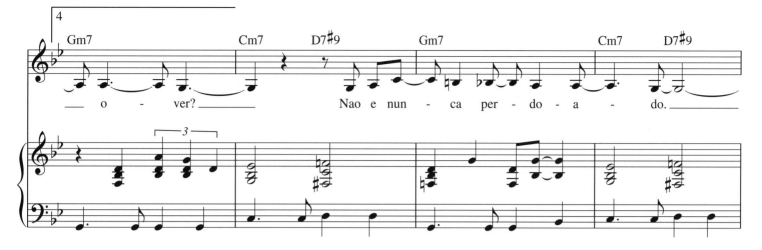

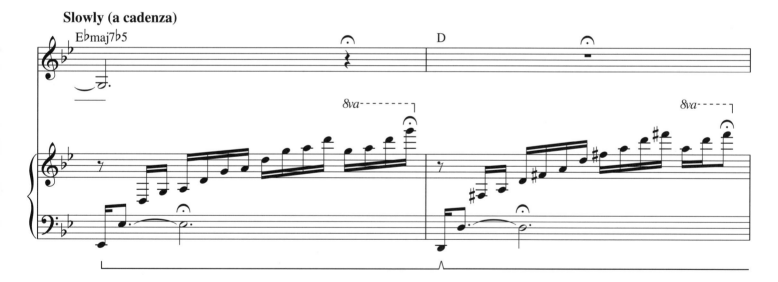

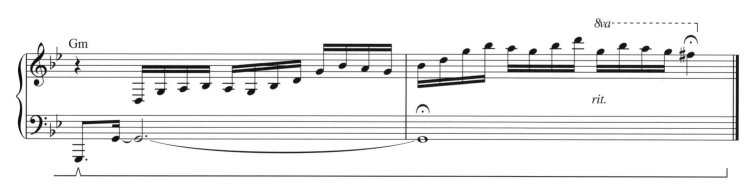

IT COULD HAPPEN TO YOU

from the Paramount Picture AND THE ANGELS SING

Words by JOHNNY BURKE
Music by JAMES VAN HEUSEN

Moderate Samba

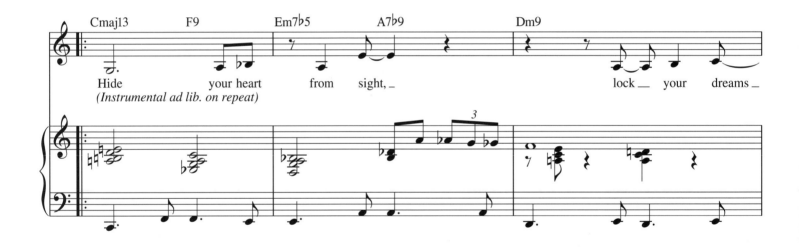

Hide your heart from sight,_ lock_ your dreams_
(Instrumental ad lib. on repeat)

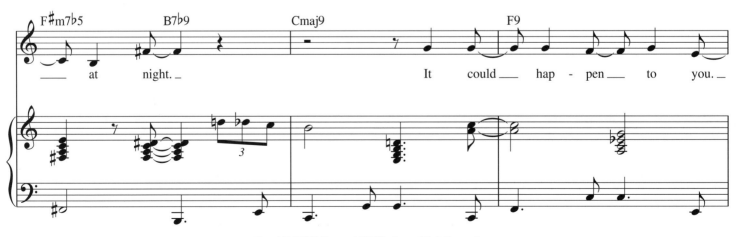

_ at night._ It could_ hap-pen_ to you._

Don't ___ count ___

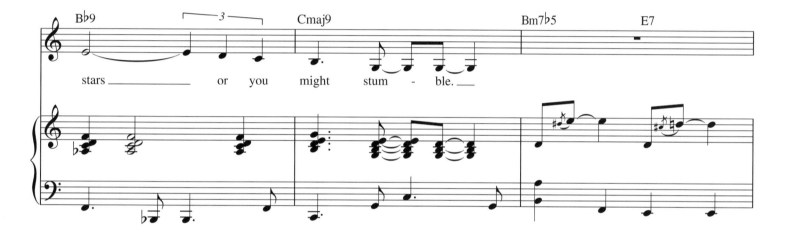

stars _____ or you might stum - ble. ___

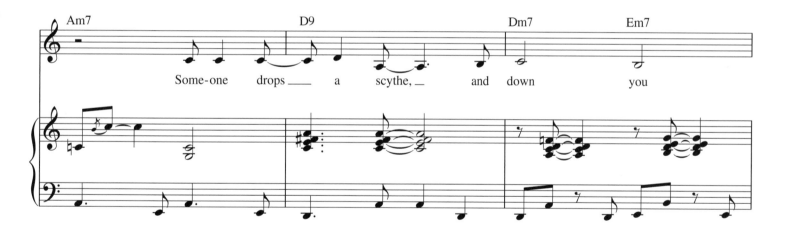

Some-one drops ___ a scythe, ___ and down you

tum - ble. Keep an eye ___ on ___ Spring,

run ___ when _____ church bells ___ ring. ___ It could ___

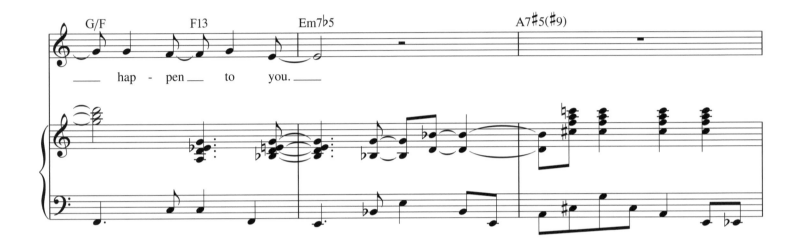

___ hap - pen ___ to you. ___

All I ev - er did ___ was won - der how ___ your arms ___ would ___

___ be, ___ then it hap - pened _ to

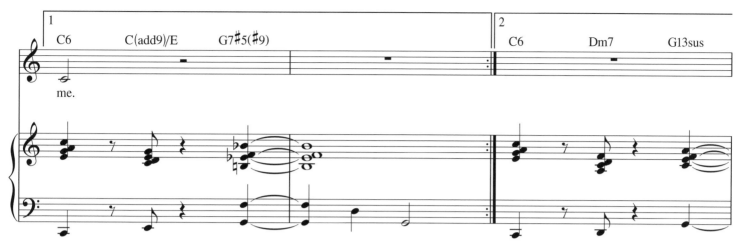

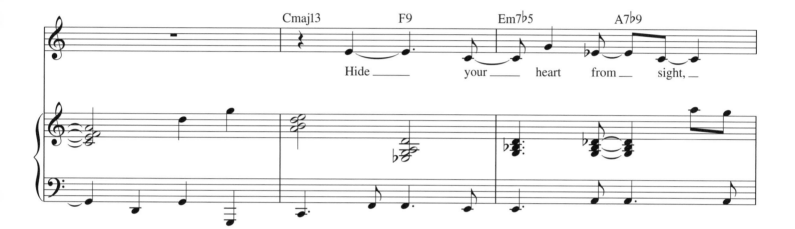

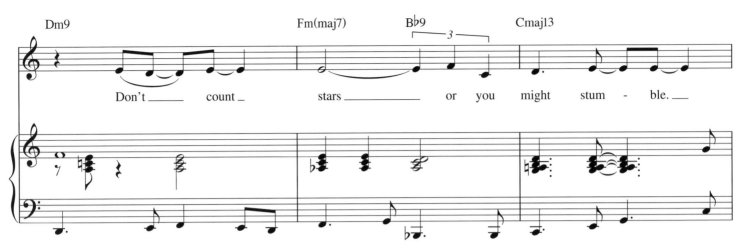

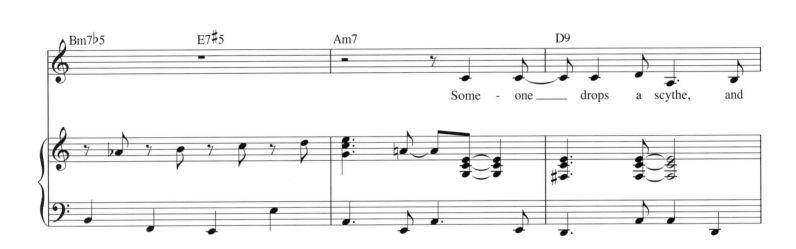

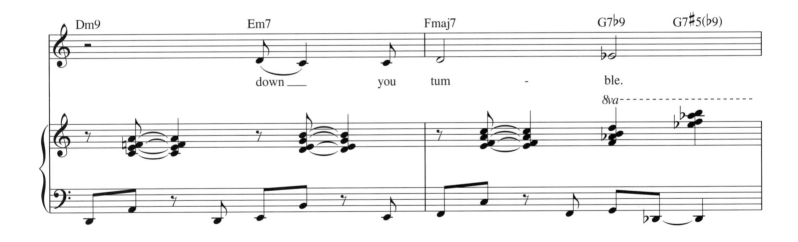

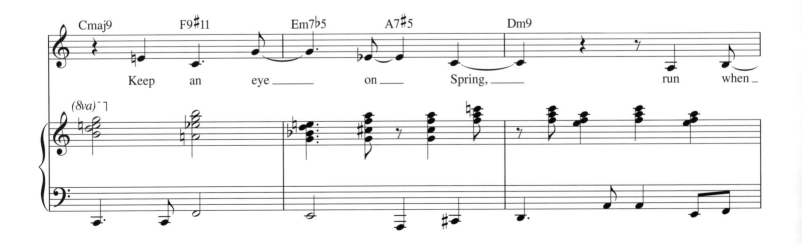

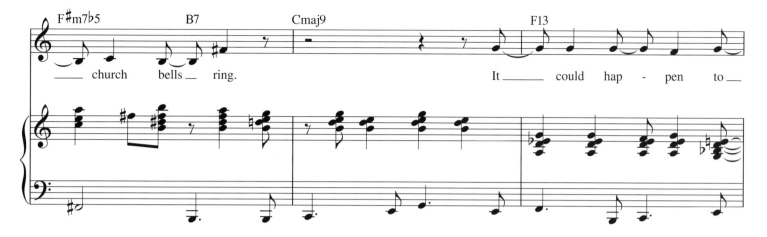

church bells _ ring. It _ could hap - pen to _

_ you. _ All I ev - er did _

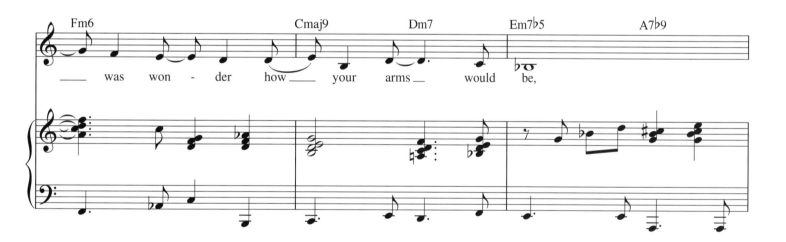

_ was won - der how _ your arms _ would be,

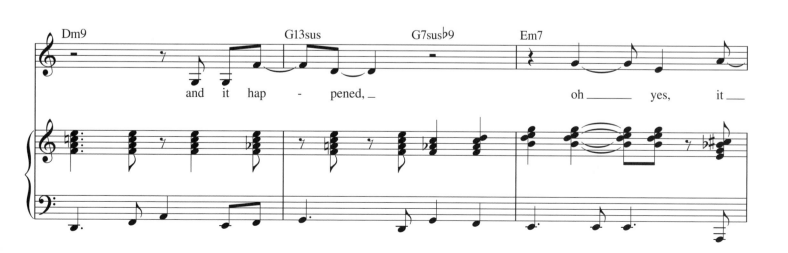

and it hap - pened, _ oh _ yes, it _

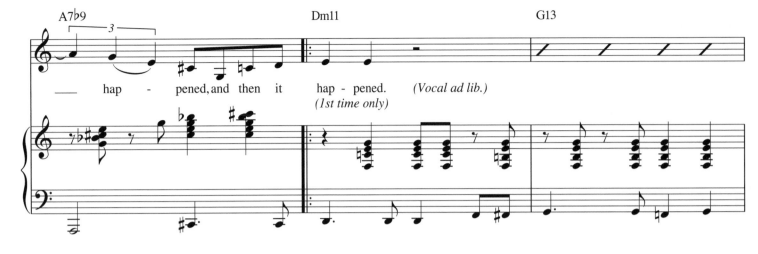

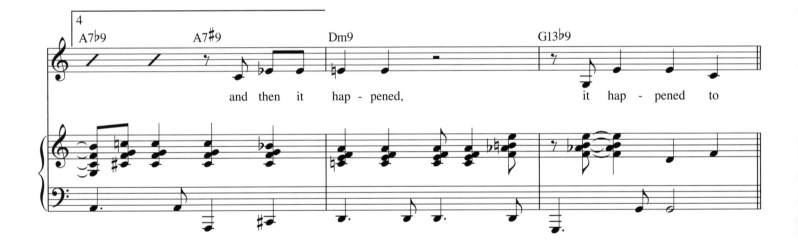

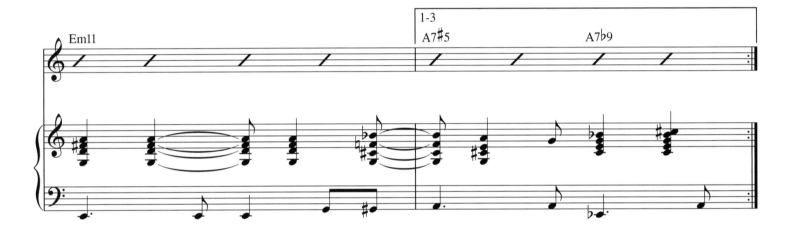

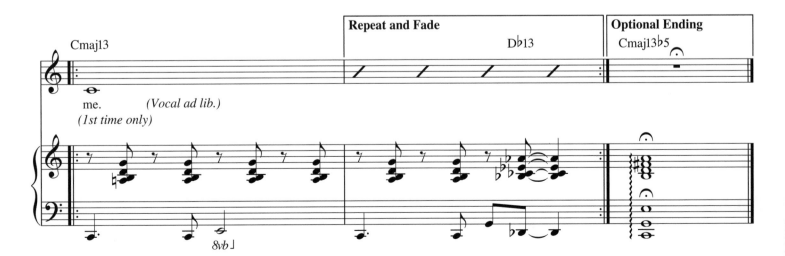

IT'S EASY TO REMEMBER
from the Paramount Picture MISSISSIPPI

Words by LORENZ HART
Music by RICHARD RODGERS

whis - per, _____ "I'll al - ways love you." _____

I know it's o - ver, and yet _____

it's eas - y to _____ re - mem - ber, _____

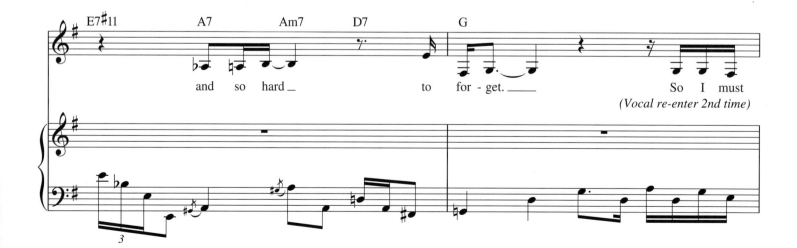

and so hard _____ to for - get. _____ So I must

(Vocal re-enter 2nd time)

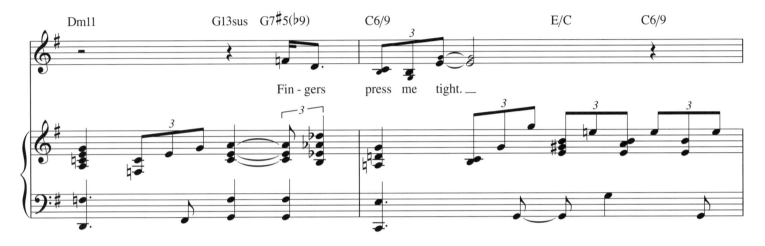

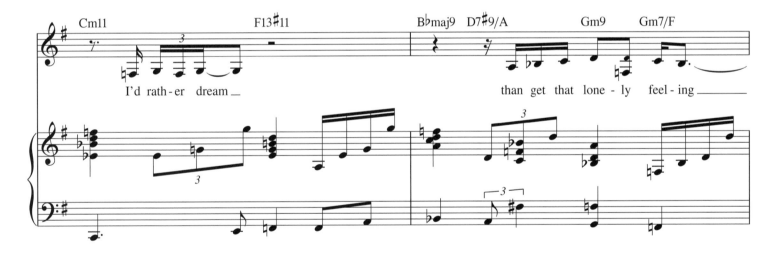

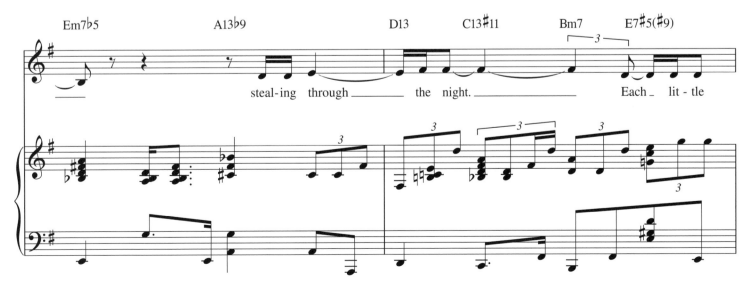

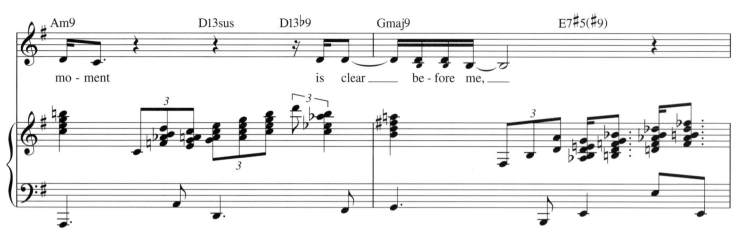

mo - ment   is   clear _____ be - fore me,

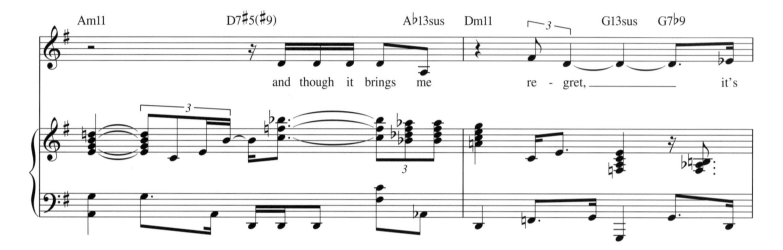

and though it brings me   re - gret, _____ it's

To Coda ⊕

eas - y _____   to re - mem - ber,

D.S. al Coda

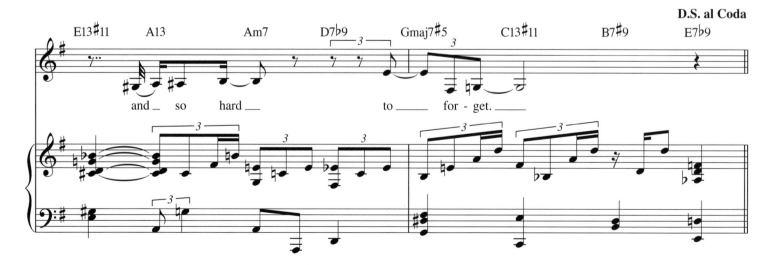

and _ so hard _____   to _____ for - get.

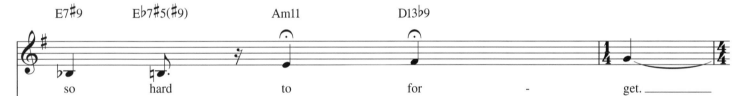

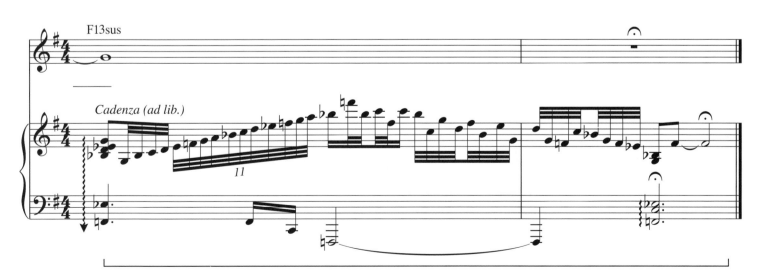

IT MIGHT AS WELL BE SPRING

from STATE FAIR

Lyrics by OSCAR HAMMERSTEIN II
Music by RICHARD RODGERS

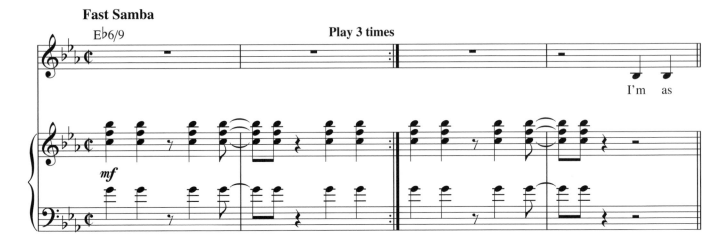

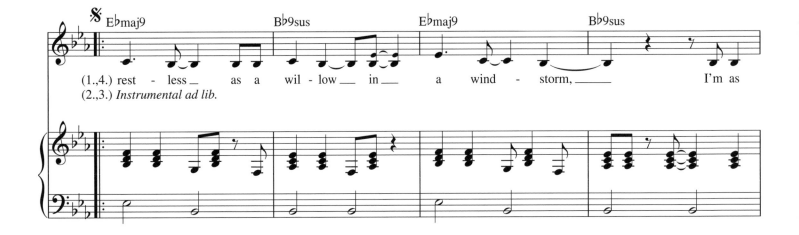

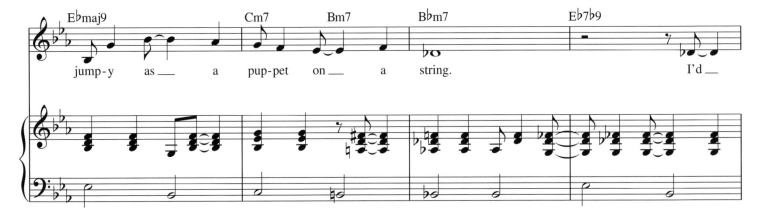

say that I had ___ Spring ___ fe - ver, when I ___

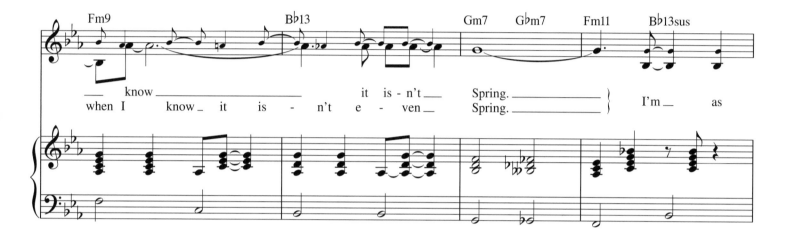

___ know ___ it is - n't ___ Spring. ___ I'm ___ as
when I know ___ it is - n't e - ven ___ Spring. ___

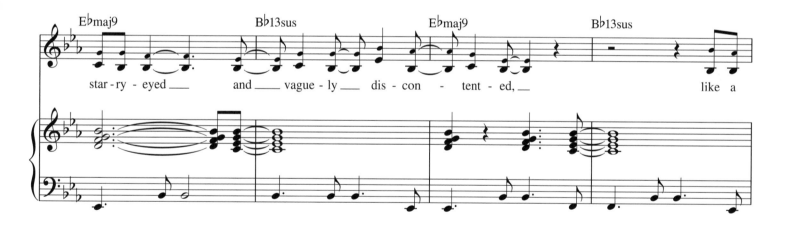

star - ry - eyed ___ and ___ vague - ly ___ dis - con - tent - ed, ___ like a

night - in - gale ___ with - out a ___ song ___ to sing. ___ Oh, ___

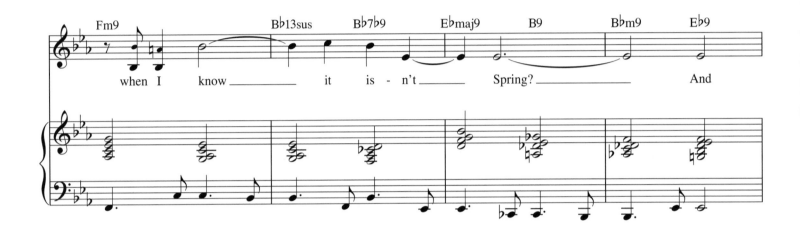

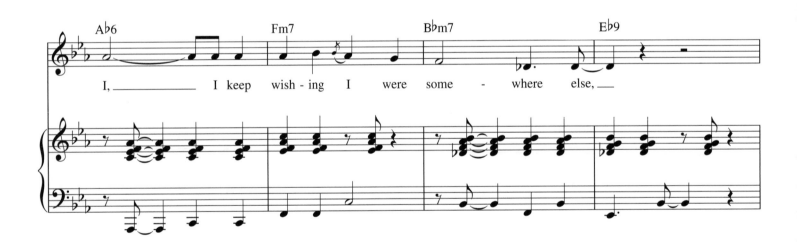

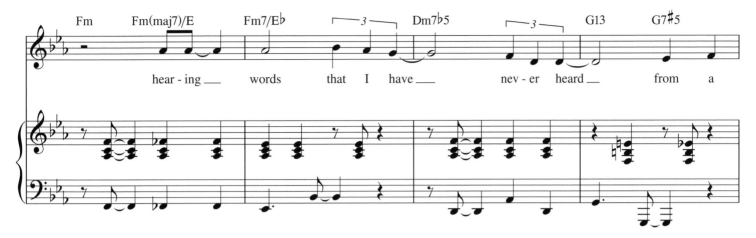

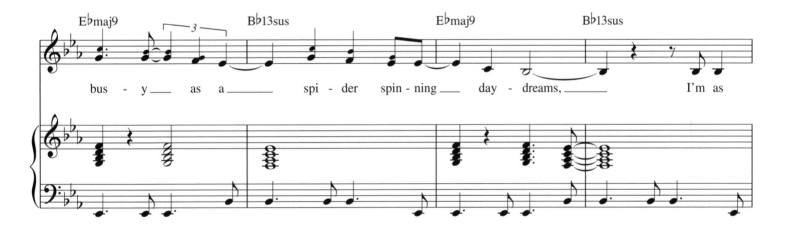

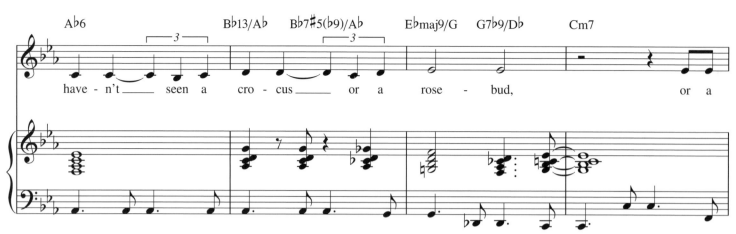

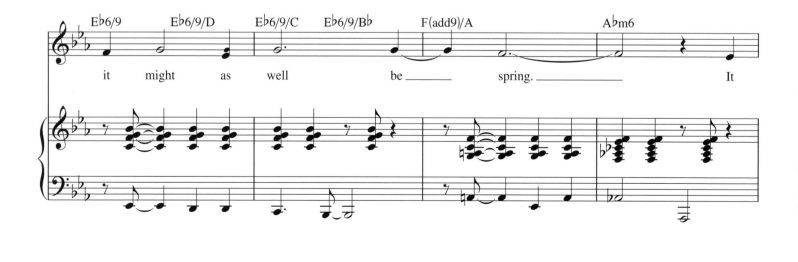

might as ____ well, might as ____ well be

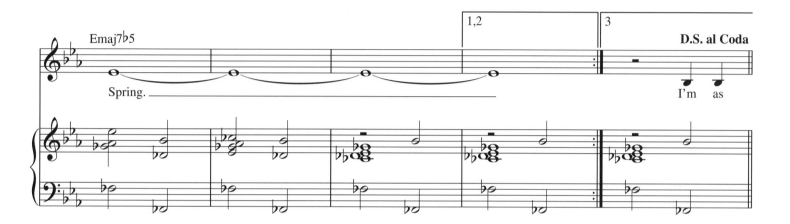

Spring. ____

I'm as

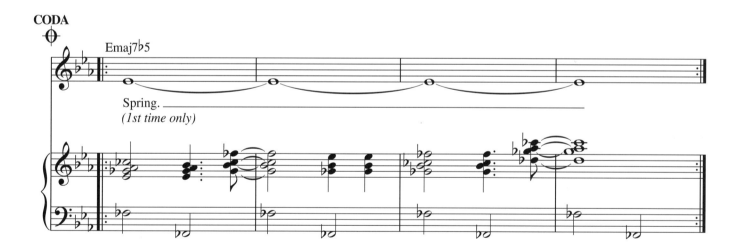

CODA

Spring. ____
(1st time only)

Repeat and Fade | **Optional Ending**

(Vocal ad lib.)

THE MOON IS A HARSH MISTRESS

Words and Music by
JIMMY WEBB

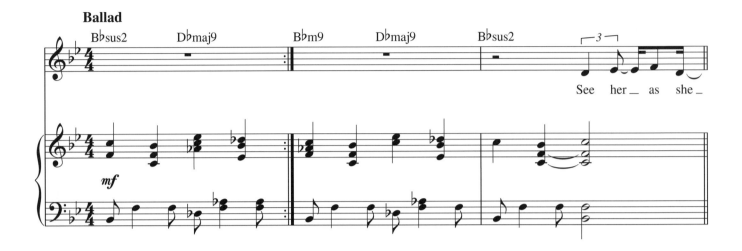

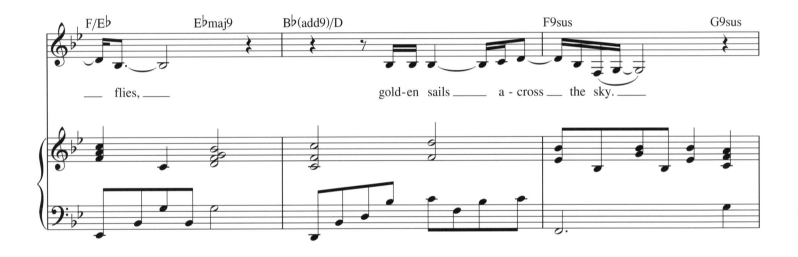

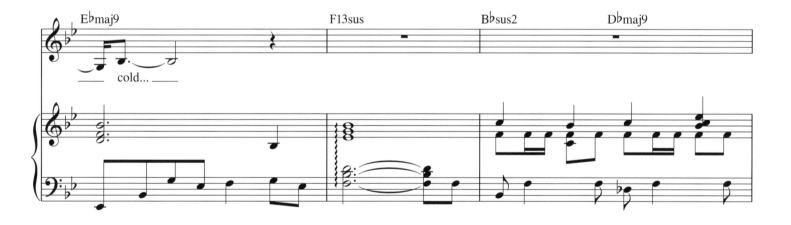

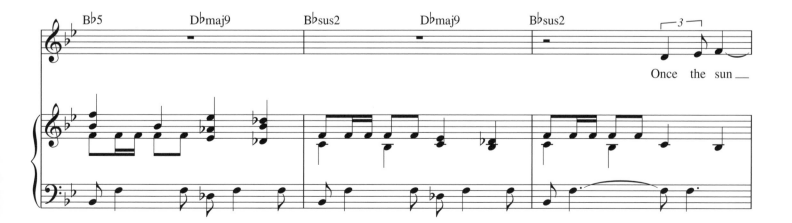

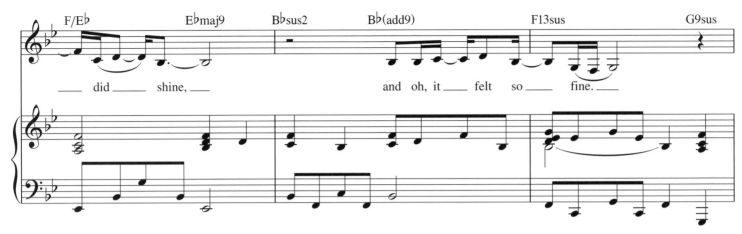

___ did ___ shine, ___ and oh, it ___ felt so ___ fine. ____

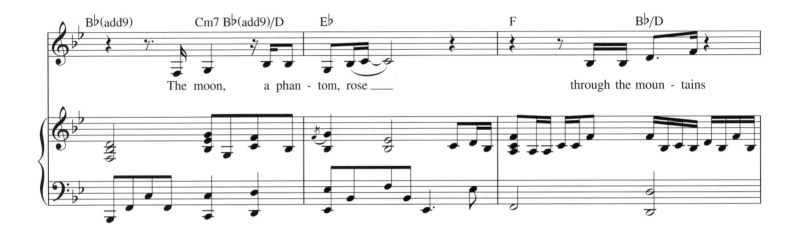

The moon, a phan - tom, rose ___ through the moun - tains

and the pines, ___ and _ then _ the dark - ness fell. ___

The moon's a harsh _____ mis - tress. __ It's hard to love her

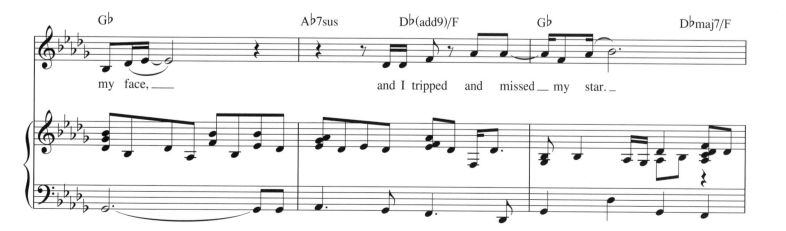

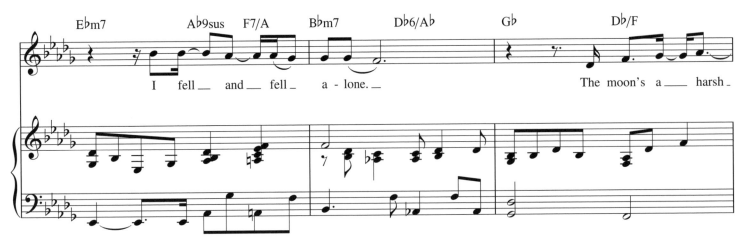

I fell __ and __ fell __ a - lone. __ The moon's a __ harsh __

__ mis - tress. __ The sky is made of __ stone. __

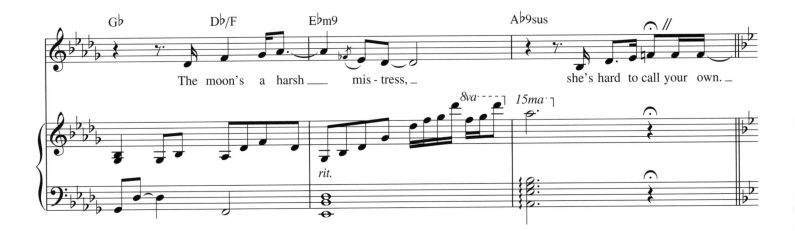

The moon's a harsh __ mis - tress, __ she's hard to call your own. __

O PATO
(The Duck)

Words and Music by JAYME SILVA
and NEUZA TEIXIERA
English Lyric by JON HENDRICKS

Moderate Samba

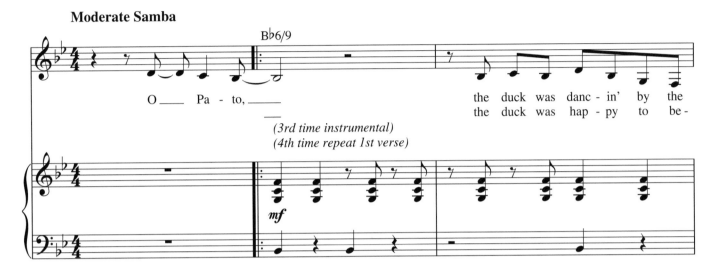

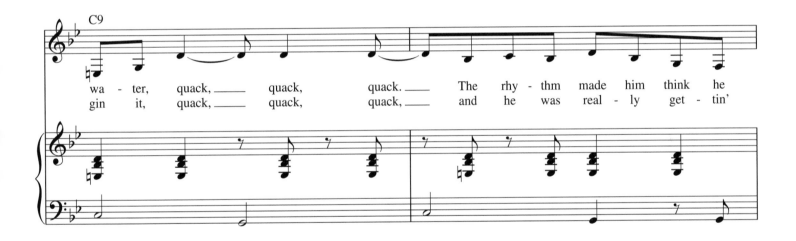

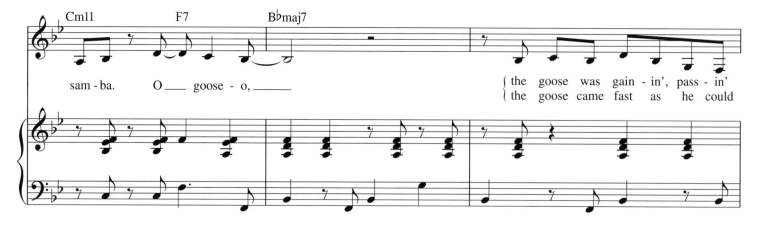

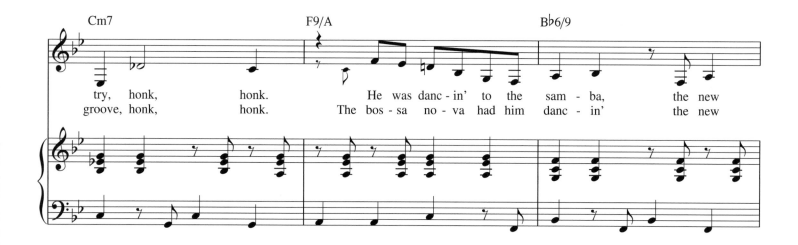

by in all her maj-es-ty, then she loos-ened up. Hoot-chie

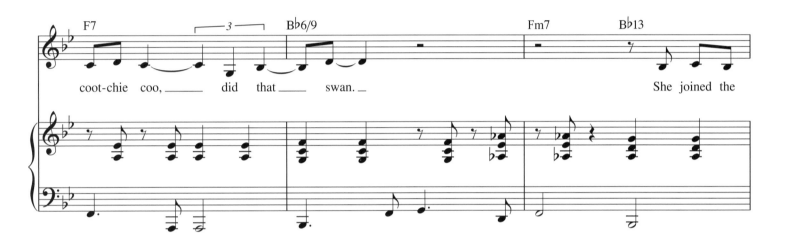

coot-chie coo, _____ did that _____ swan. _____ She joined the

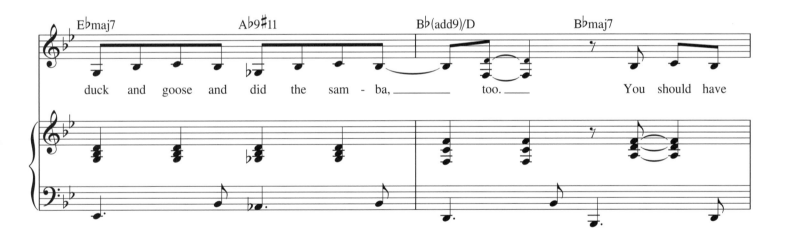

duck and goose and did the sam - ba, _____ too. _____ You should have

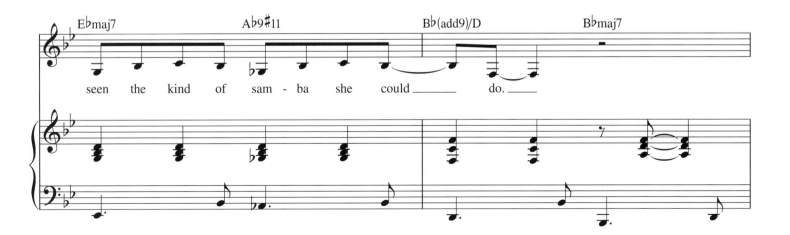

seen the kind of sam-ba she could _____ do. _____

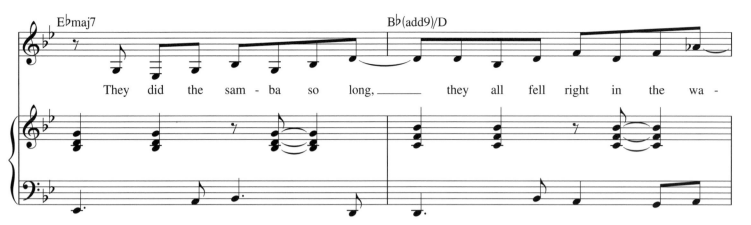

They did the sam - ba so long, _____ they all fell right in the wa -

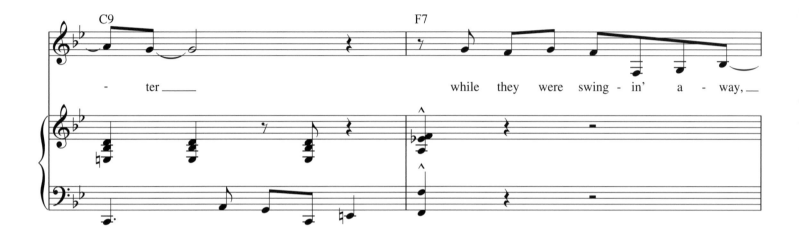

- ter _____ while they were swing - in' a - way, _____

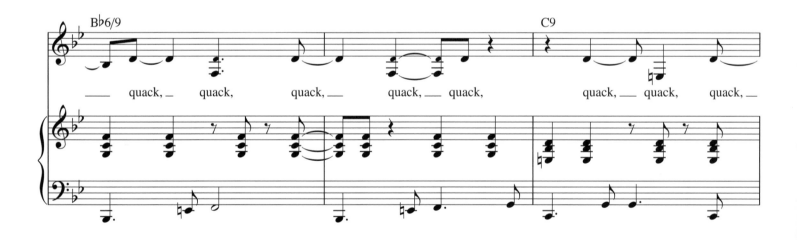

_____ quack, _____ quack, _____ quack, _____ quack, _____ quack, _____ quack, _____ quack, _____ quack, _____

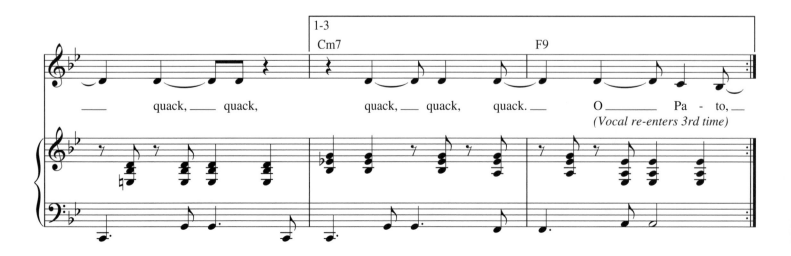

_____ quack, _____ quack, _____ quack, _____ quack, _____ quack. _____ O _____ Pa - to, _____

(Vocal re-enters 3rd time)

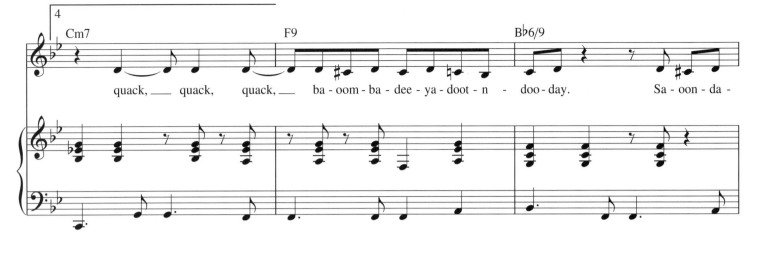

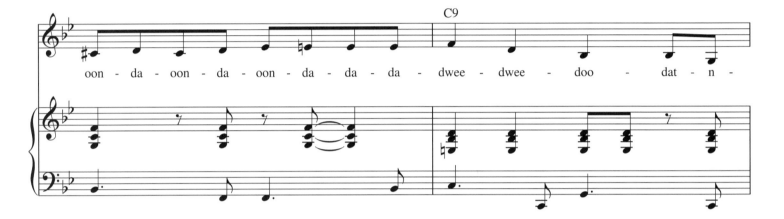

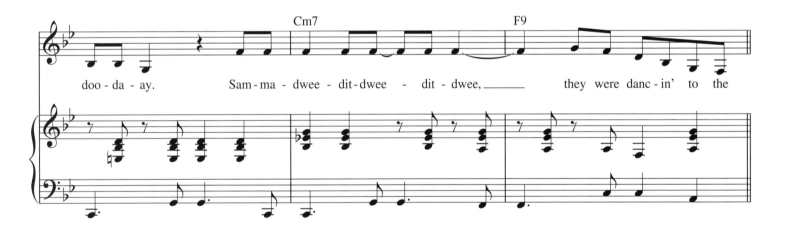

SWEET HOME COOKIN' MAN

Words and Music by
KARRIN ALLYSON

Moderate 12/8 Blues feel

Well, he ain't got per-son-al-i-ty, and he ain't got such good looks. When I come home hun-gry, Lord, how my ba-by cooks. He's a chef of fine dis-tinc-tion, al-ways cooks it up just right wheth-er I

come home in the morn - in', ba - by, or stum-ble in ___ late at ___ night. ___

Well, he might be cook-in' lob - ster, or he might be fix - in' ___ fish.

Does-n't mat - ter, dar - lin', it's al - ways the per - fect dish. ___

He's a cul - in - ar - y won - der, babe, al - ways cooks with the right ___

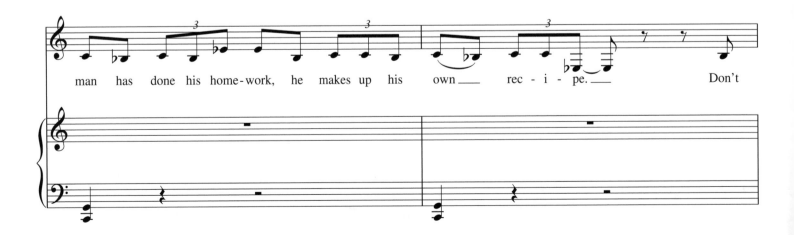

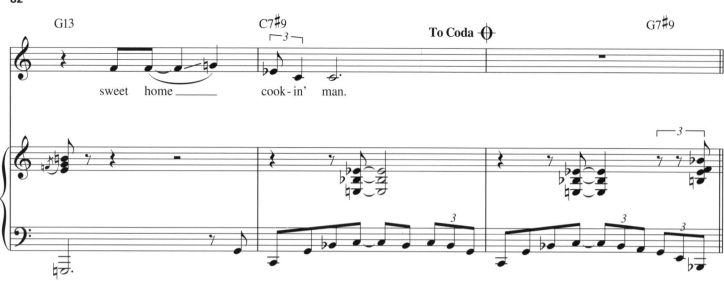

sweet home _____ cook-in' man.

(Instrumental ad lib.)

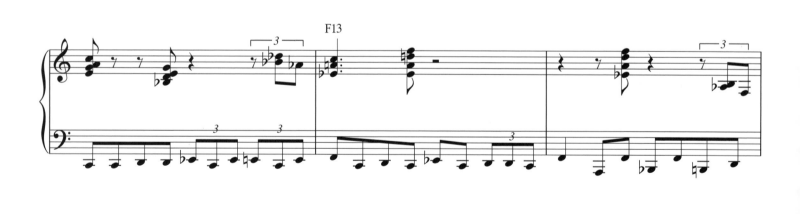

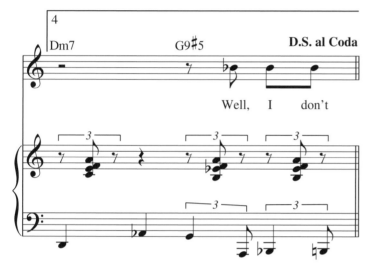

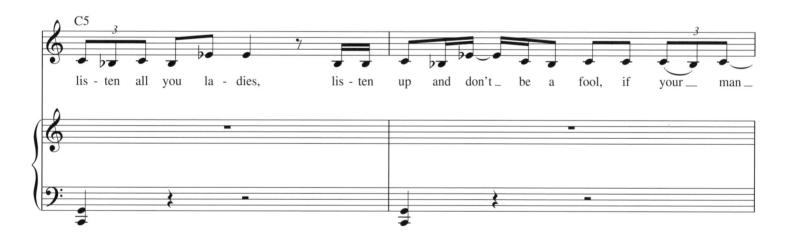

Well, I don't

So, _____

lis - ten all you la - dies, lis - ten up and don't _ be a fool, if your _ man _

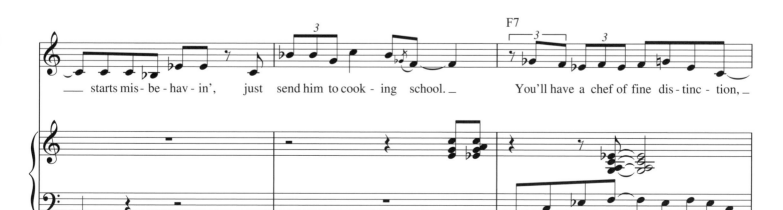

_ starts mis - be - hav - in', just send him to cook - ing school. _ You'll have a chef of fine dis - tinc - tion, _

C7#9

yes, he'll come ___ com - plete ___ with pots and ___

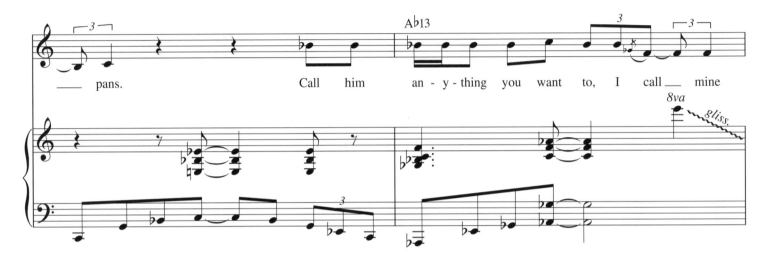

A♭13

___ pans. Call him an - y - thing you want to, I call ___ mine

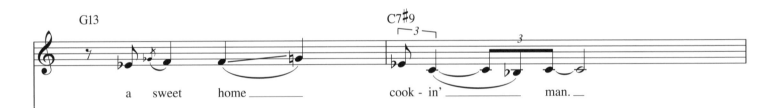

G13   C7#9

a sweet home ___ cook - in' ___ man. ___

Repeat 7 times

(Sweet...home...cookin' man...)
Vocal ad lib.

Sha - doo - day. ___

TOO YOUNG TO GO STEADY

Words and Music by JIMMY McHUGH
and HAROLD ADAMSON

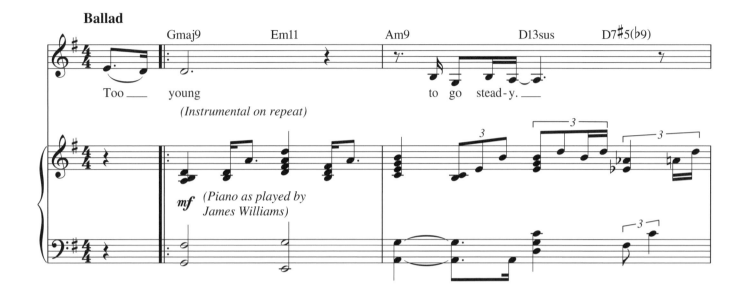

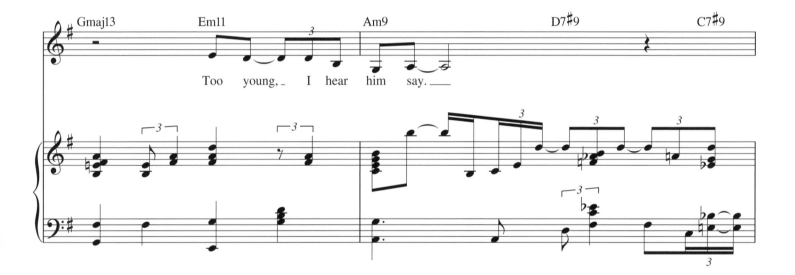

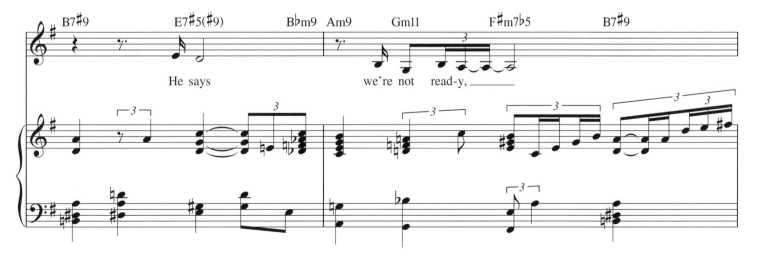

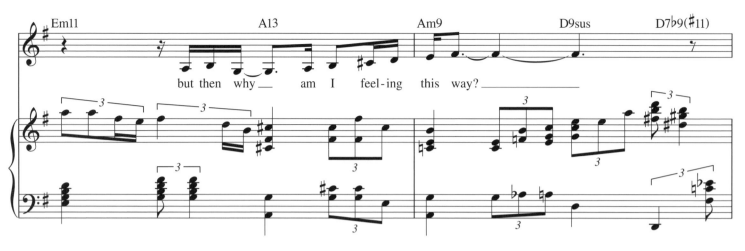

but then why___ am I feel-ing this way? ___

Too young, ___ so ___ he tells me.

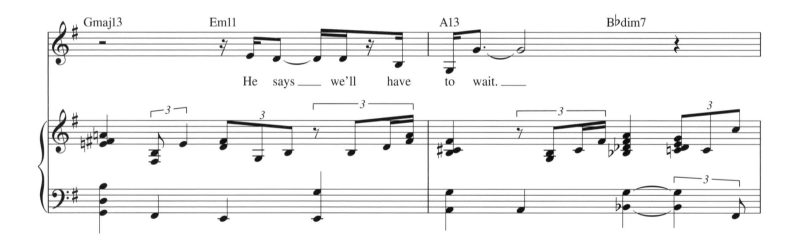

He says ___ we'll have to wait. ___

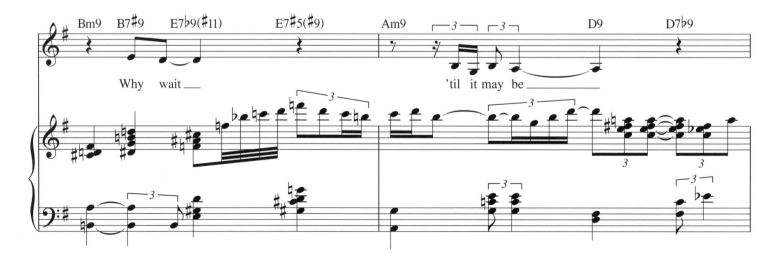

Why wait ___ 'til it may be ___

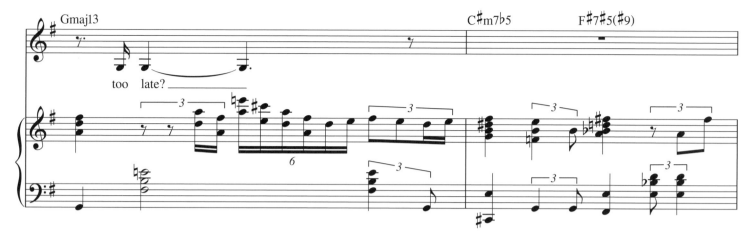

too late?

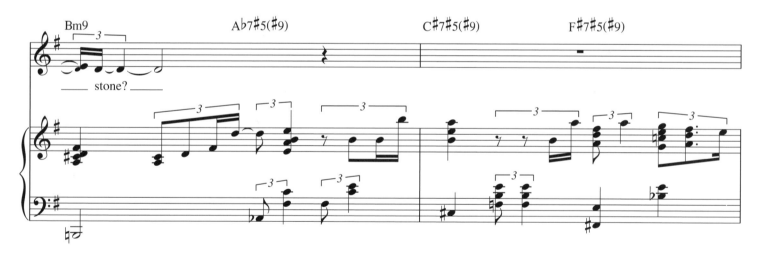

Can't he see he ___ drives me wild? _____ Is he ___ made ___ of ___
(Vocal re-enters on repeat)

___ stone? _____

Must he al - ways ___ treat me like a child? _____ Won't he ev - er own ___

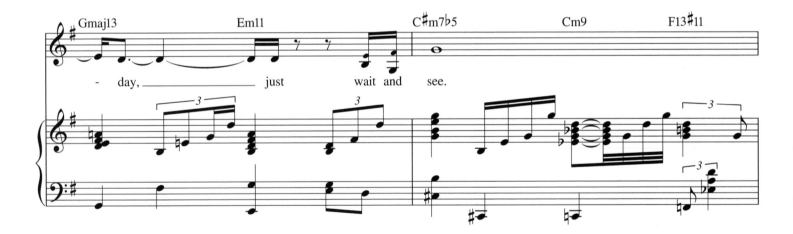

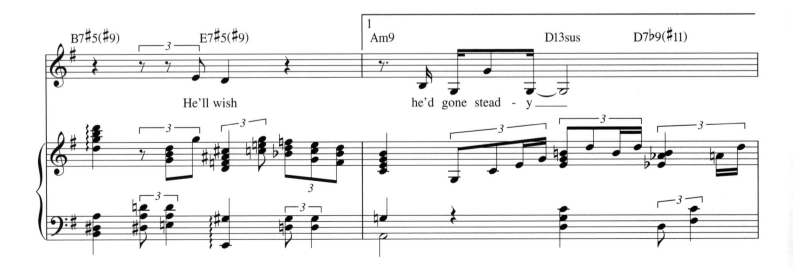

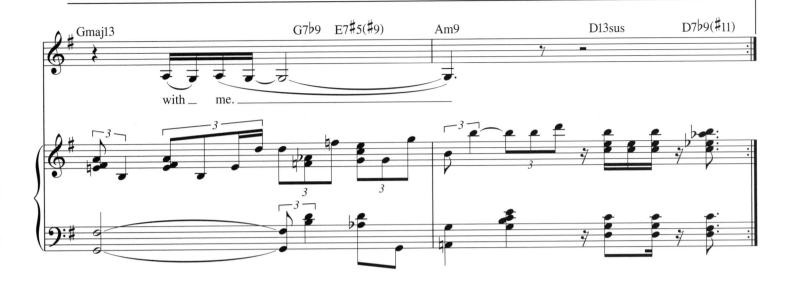

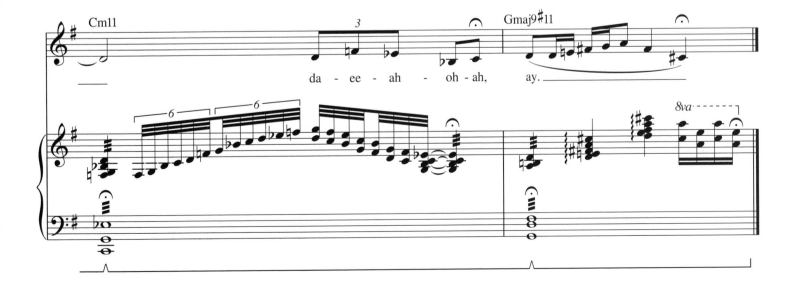

YOU ARE TOO BEAUTIFUL

from HALLELUHAH, I'M A BUM

Words by LORENZ HART
Music by RICHARD RODGERS

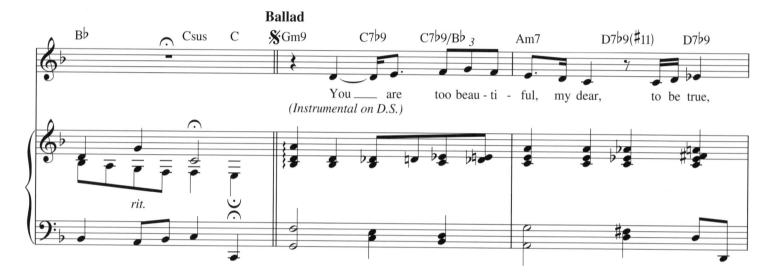

I could have bound ___ you, too. You are too beau -

ti-ful for just one ___ a - lone, ___ for one ___ luck-y fool _____ to be with

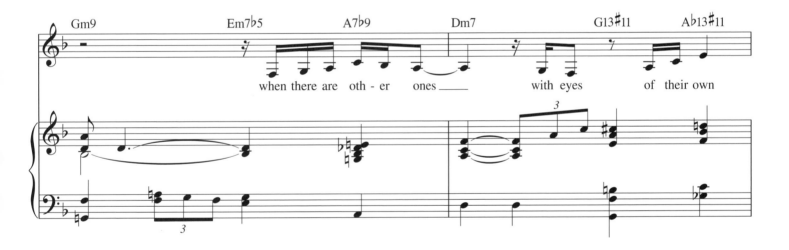

when there are oth - er ones _____ with eyes of their own

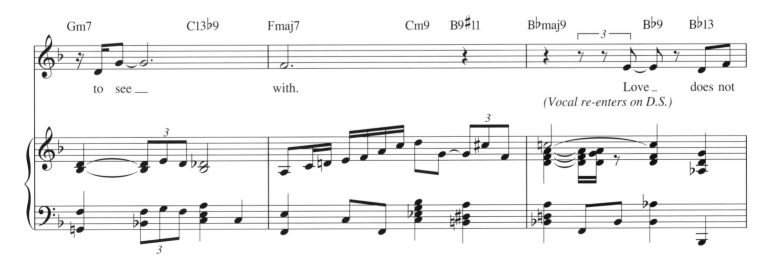

to see ___ with. Love ___ does not
(Vocal re-enters on D.S.)

stand shar-ing, __ not if some - one __ real-ly cares.

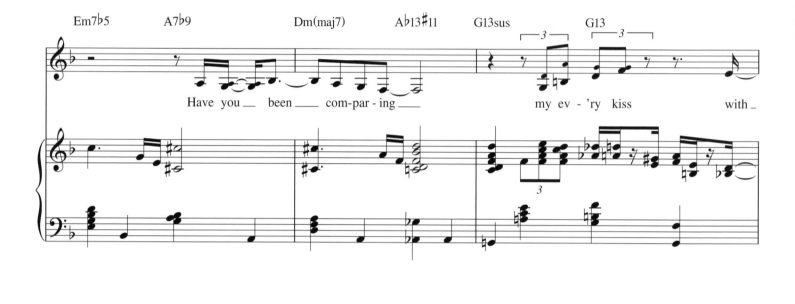

Have you __ been __ com-par-ing __ my ev-'ry kiss with __

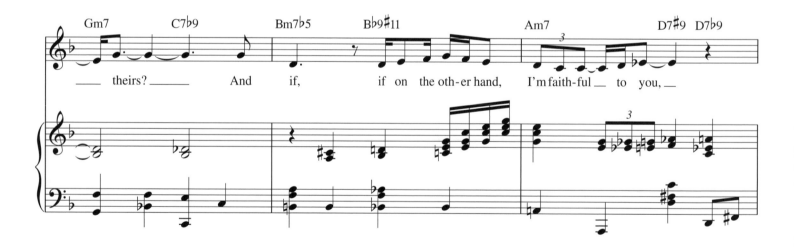

__ theirs? __ And if, if on the oth-er hand, I'm faith-ful __ to you, __

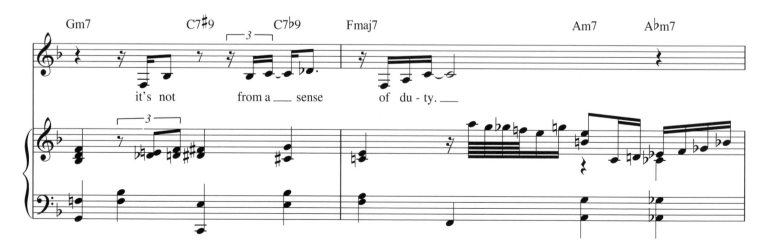

it's not from a __ sense of du-ty. __

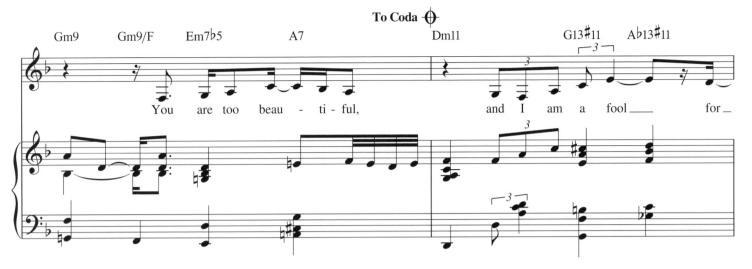

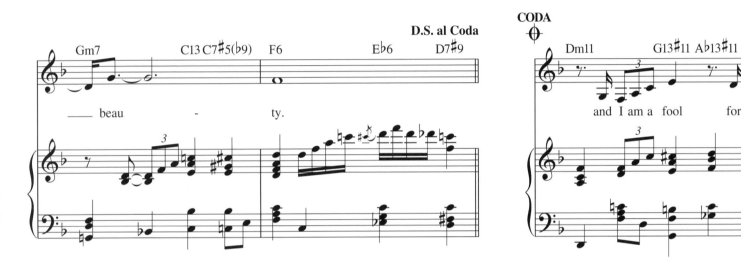

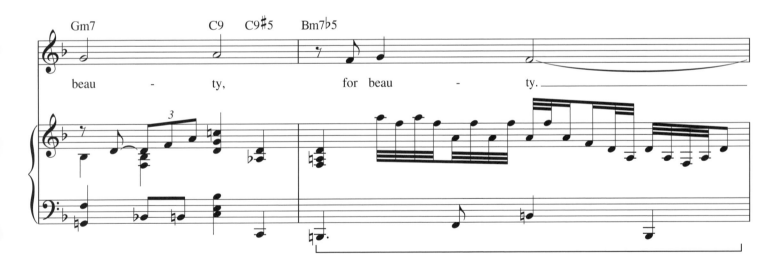

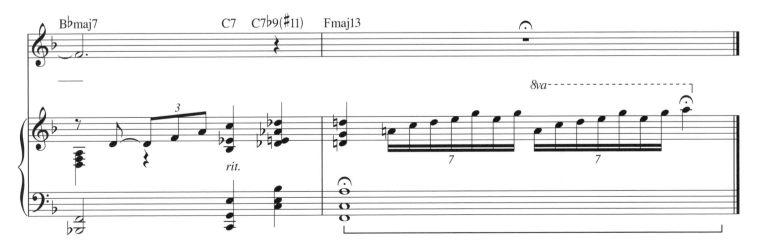

discography

And So It Goes – Collage *(Concord Jazz 4709)*
Arranged by Bill McGlaughlin

Angel Eyes – In Blue *(Concord Jazz 2106)*
Arranged by Danny Embrey

Azure Té (Paris Blues) – Azure-Te *(Concord Jazz 4641)*
Arranged by Rod Fleeman

Blame It on My Youth – Azure-Te *(Concord Jazz 4641)*

Daydream – Daydream *(Concord Jazz 4773)*
Arranged by Karrin Allyson

Feel Like Makin' Love – Wild for You *(Concord Jazz 1222)*
Arranged by Gil Goldstein

Here, There and Everywhere – Collage *(Concord Jazz 4709)*
Arranged by Bob Bowman

How Insensitive – I Didn't Know about You *(Concord Jazz 4543)*
Arranged by Bill McGlaughlin and Karrin Allyson

It Could Happen to You – Collage *(Concord Jazz 4709)*
Arranged by Danny Embrey

It Might as Well Be Spring – I Didn't Know about You *(Concord Jazz 4543)*
Arranged by Danny Embrey

It's Easy to Remember – Ballads: Remembering John Coltrane *(Concord Jazz 4950)*

The Moon Is a Harsh Mistress – Wild for You *(Concord Jazz 1222)*
Arranged by Gil Goldstein

O Pato (The Duck) – From Paris to Rio *(Concord Jazz 4865)*
Arranged by Danny Embrey

Sweet Home Cookin' Man – Sweet Home Cookin' *(Concord Jazz 4593)*

Too Young to Go Steady – Ballads: Remembering John Coltrane *(Concord Jazz 4950)*

You Are Too Beautiful – Sweet Home Cookin' *(Concord Jazz 4593)*
Arranged by Alan Broadbent

ARTIST TRANSCRIPTIONS

Artist Transcriptions are authentic, note-for-note transcriptions of the hottest artists in jazz, pop, and rock today. These outstanding, accurate arrangements are in an easy-to-read format which includes all essential lines. Artist Transcriptions can be used to perform, sequence or reference.

GUITAR & BASS

George Benson
00660113 Guitar Style of $14.95

Pierre Bensusan
00699072 Guitar Book of................$19.95

Ron Carter
00672331 Acoustic Bass................$16.95

Stanley Clarke
00672307 The Collection................$19.95

Al Di Meola
00604041 Cielo E Terra $14.95
00660115 Friday Night in
             San Francisco..............$14.95
00604043 Music, Words, Pictures....$14.95

Tal Farlow
00673245 Jazz Style of $19.95

Bela Fleck and the Flecktones
00672359 Melody/Lyrics/Chords......$18.95

Frank Gambale
00672336 Best of $22.95

Jim Hall
00699389 Jazz Guitar Environments ..$19.95
00699306 Exploring Jazz Guitar $17.95

Allan Holdsworth
00604049 Reaching for the
             Uncommon Chord $14.95

Leo Kottke
00699215 Eight Songs $14.95

Wes Montgomery
00675536 Guitar Transcriptions $17.95

Joe Pass
00672353 The Collection................$18.95

John Patitucci
00673216 ....$14.95

Django Reinhardt
00027083 Anthology $14.95
00026711 The Genius of $10.95
00026715 A Treasury of Songs $12.95

Johnny Smith
00672374 Guitar Solos $16.95

Mike Stern
00673224 Guitar Book....................$16.95

Mark Whitfield
00672320 Guitar Collection $19.95

Gary Willis
00672337 The Collection................$19.95

SAXOPHONE

Julian "Cannonball" Adderley
00673244 The Collection................$19.95

Michael Brecker
00673237 ....$19.95
00672429 The Collection................$19.95

The Brecker Brothers
00672351 And All Their Jazz...........$19.95
00672447 Best of $19.95

Benny Carter
00672314 The Collection................$22.95
00672315 Plays Standards $22.95

James Carter
00672394 The Collection................$19.95

John Coltrane
00672494 A Love Supreme.............$12.95
00672529 Giant Steps....................$14.95
00672493 Plays Coltrane Changes..$19.95
00672349 Plays Giant Steps $19.95
00672453 Plays Standards $19.95
00673233 Solos............................$22.95

Paul Desmond
00672328 The Collection................$19.95
00672454 Standard Time $19.95

Kenny Garrett
00672530 The Collection................$19.95

Stan Getz
00699375 ....$18.95
00672377 Bossa Novas $19.95
00672375 Standards $17.95

Coleman Hawkins
00672523 The Collection................$19.95

Joe Henderson
00672330 Best of $22.95
00673252 Selections from Lush Life
             & So Near So Far $19.95

Kenny G
00673239 Best of $19.95
00673229 Breathless....................$19.95
00672462 Classics in the Key of G ..$19.95
00672485 Faith: A Holiday Album....$14.95
00672373 The Moment $19.95
00672516 Paradise $14.95

Joe Lovano
00672326 The Collection................$19.95

Jackie McLean
00672498 The Collection................$19.95

James Moody
00672372 The Collection................$19.95

Frank Morgan
00672416 The Collection................$19.95

Sonny Rollins
00672444 The Collection................$19.95

David Sanborn
00675000 The Collection................$16.95

Bud Shank
00672528 The Collection................$19.95

Wayne Shorter
00672498 New Best of $19.95

Lew Tabackin
00672455 The Collection................$19.95

Stanley Turrentine
00672334 The Collection................$19.95

Lester Young
00672524 The Collection................$19.95

PIANO & KEYBOARD

Monty Alexander
00672338 The Collection................$19.95
00672487 Plays Standards $19.95

Kenny Barron
00672318 The Collection................$22.95

Count Basie
00672520 The Collection................$19.95

Warren Bernhardt
00672364 The Collection................$19.95

Cyrus Chesnut
00672439 The Collection................$19.95

Billy Childs
00673242 The Collection................$19.95

Chick Corea
00672300 Paint the World $12.95

Bill Evans
00672537 At Town Hall $16.95
00672365 The Collection................$19.95
00672425 Piano Interpretations........$19.95
00672510 Trio, Vol. 1: 1959-1961 ....$24.95
00672511 Trio, Vol. 2: 1962-1965 ....$24.95
00672512 Trio, Vol. 3: 1968-1974 ....$24.95
00672513 Trio, Vol. 4: 1979-1980 ....$24.95

Benny Goodman
00672492 The Collection................$16.95

Benny Green
00672329 The Collection................$19.95

Vince Guaraldi
00672486 The Collection................$19.95

Herbie Hancock
00672419 The Collection................$19.95

Gene Harris
00672446 The Collection................$19.95

Hampton Hawes
00672438 The Collection................$19.95

Ahmad Jamal
00672322 The Collection................$22.95

CLARINET

Buddy De Franco
00672423 The Collection................$19.95

FLUTE

Eric Dolphy
00672379 The Collection................$19.95

James Moody
00672372 The Collection $19.95

James Newton
00660108 Improvising Flute $14.95

Lew Tabackin
00672455 The Collection................$19.95

TROMBONE

J.J. Johnson
00672332 The Collection................$19.95

Brad Mehldau
00672476 The Collection................$19.95

Thelonious Monk
00672388 Best of $19.95
00672389 The Collection................$19.95
00672390 Jazz Standards, Vol. 1 ....$19.95
00672391 Jazz Standards, Vol. 2 ....$19.95
00672392 Intermediate Piano Solos..$14.95

Jelly Roll Morton
00672433 The Piano Rolls..............$12.95

Oscar Peterson
00672531 Plays Duke Ellington........$19.95
00672534 Very Best of $19.95

Michael Petrucciani
00673226 ....$17.95

Bud Powell
00672371 Classics $19.95
00672376 The Collection................$19.95

André Previn
00672437 The Collection................$19.95

Gonzalo Rubalcaba
00672507 The Collection................$19.95

Horace Silver
00672303 The Collection................$19.95

Art Tatum
00672316 The Collection................$22.95
00672355 Solo Book $19.95

Billy Taylor
00672357 The Collection................$24.95

McCoy Tyner
00673215 ....$16.95

Cedar Walton
00672321 The Collection................$19.95

Kenny Werner
00672519 The Collection................$19.95

Teddy Wilson
00672434 The Collection................$19.95

TRUMPET

Louis Armstrong
00672480 The Collection................$14.95
00672481 Plays Standards $14.95

Chet Baker
00672435 The Collection................$19.95

Randy Brecker
00673234 ....$17.95

The Brecker Brothers
00672351 And All Their Jazz...........$19.95
00672447 Best of $19.95

Miles Davis
00672448 Originals, Vol. 1 ....$19.95
00672451 Originals, Vol. 2 ....$19.95
00672450 Standards, Vol. 1 ....$19.95
00672449 Standards, Vol. 2 ....$19.95

Dizzy Gillespie
00672479 The Collection................$19.95

Freddie Hubbard
00673214 ....$14.95

Tom Harrell
00672382 Jazz Trumpet Solos $19.95

Chuck Mangione
00672506 The Collection................$19.95